THE Holocaust

Editor
Geoffrey Wigoder

A
Grolier Student
Library

Volume 3
Macedonia to Szenes

Grolier Educational

SHERMAN TURNPIKE, DANBURY, CONNECTICUT

Concept, Content and Editorial Advisor
Charles E. Smith

Managing Editor
Rachel Gilon

Library of Congress Cataloging-in-Publication Data

The Holocaust.
    p.   cm.
   Summary. Articles identify and describe individuals and events
connected with the persecution of Jews and others across Europe in
the 1930s and 1940s.
  ISBN 0-7172-7637-6
  1. Holocaust , Jewish (1939-1945)—Encyclopedias, Juvenile.
[1. Holocaust , Jewish (1939-1945)—Encyclopedias.]
D804.25.H65   1996
940.53'18'03—dc20

96-9566
CIP
AC

Published 1997 by Grolier Educational,
Sherman Turnpike, Danbury, Connecticut
© 1997 by Charles E. Smith Books, Inc.

Set ISBN 0-7172-7637-6
Volume 3: ISBN 0-7172-7640-6

For information, address the publisher:
Grolier Educational, Sherman Turnpike, Danbury, Connecticut 06816

Cover design by Smart Graphics
Planned and produced by The Jerusalem Publishing House, Jerusalem
Printed in Hong Kong

M

MACEDONIA

see YUGOSLAVIA.

MADAGASCAR PLAN

A plan designed by Adolf EICHMANN before WORLD WAR II to deport the JEWS of Europe to the island of Madagascar, a French colony located off the southeast coast of Africa. Like much of Nazi policy against the Jews, this plan was not original. The original suggestion to deport the Jews of Europe to Madagascar was made by Paul de Lagarde, a French antisemite, in 1885 as part of his solution to rid Europe of the "Jewish Problem." There were other similar proposals to use Madagascar as the resettling point for Jews. In 1937, a Polish commission even visited the island to examine its potential for absorbing the Jews of Europe.

In March 1938, Eichmann began a preliminary report on Madagascar. In 1940, he prepared a detailed plan for the evacuation of 4 million Jews to the island to be carried out over a period of four years. He called it a "gross ghetto," meaning a giant ghetto. The plan was to be funded by money raised from the sale of confiscated Jewish properties (see ARYANIZATION) and from other Jewish contributions. Eichmann informed the leaders of German Jewry of the intention to deport them to Madagascar, but they reacted by saying that the only acceptable destination for them would be PALESTINE. The Madagascar Plan became impractical later in the year when Germany

The crematoria at Majdanek with piles of bones in front of them

Uniforms worn by prisoners in the camp displayed in the Majdanek Museum

lost the Battle of Britain, and the idea of transporting 4 million Jews to the Indian Ocean became a pipe dream.

Some scholars suggest that the true purpose of the plan was to hide the real intention of the Nazis—to murder the Jews of Europe. Others say that the Madagascar Plan shows that the "FINAL SOLUTION" had not yet evolved.

MAJDANEK

DEATH CAMP located in a suburb of LUBLIN, POLAND. In Majdanek, 360,000 people were shot, beaten, starved or gassed to death. Their bodies were then buried in mass graves or burned in a crematorium.

The camp was composed of five sections with 144 barracks. It housed up to 45,000 prisoners. It was originally built in the winter of 1940–1941 to house prisoners of war. Russian prisoners were brought there beginning in July 1941. It soon became a camp for Jews and Poles as well.

The victims of Majdanek included between 100,000 and 150,000 Jews from Poland and western Europe, over 100,000 non-Jewish Poles, and tens of thousands of Russian prisoners of war. Most died from exposure, starvation, exhaustion, disease, and the harsh conditions. The great majority of those murdered in the GAS CHAMBERS were Jews. The worst massacre occurred on 3 November 1943, when 18,000 Jews were murdered in a single day. They were shot in pits while loudspeakers played dance music to drown out the sounds. This day was called the ERNTEFEST (the harvest festival) by the Germans.

Majdanek was liberated on 24 July 1944 by the Soviet army. At that time, only a few hundred Jewish inmates were still alive.

Today, Majdanek is one of the best preserved camps. Several major sections are still intact. They house a museum that pays tribute to those who were murdered there. Original gas chambers and crematoria still stand on the highest hill of the camp. Next to the gas chamber building is a huge mound of ashes from the crematoria, sheltered by a dome-shaped roof.

MARCH OF THE LIVING

see YOUTH PILGRIMAGES TO HOLOCAUST SITES.

M A U R I T I U S

Island in the Indian Ocean where 1,580 refugees landed in December 1940.

In November 1940, 4,000 refugees—including many CHILDREN—fleeing from Nazi-occupied Europe left the Romanian port of Tulcea on the Black Sea on three Greek ships flying a Panamanian flag: the *Atlantic*, the *Pacific* and the *Milos*. Passengers had to remain below deck in order not to be seen. Conditions were so bad that many people died during the voyage. The *Atlantic* reached Haifa, PALESTINE (Israel), on 24 November, but British authorities refused to let its passengers disembark. They were told they would be transferred to another ship, the PATRIA, together with the passengers of the *Milos*

Camp newspaper of the Mauritius internees

and the *Pacific*, who had arrived earlier. The transfer was getting underway when the *Patria* sank—on 25 November. The survivors were then allowed to land, together with the other passengers of the *Atlantic*, and were imprisoned by the British army in the REFUGEE camp, Athlit, near Haifa. On 8 December, the former *Atlantic* passengers were told that they would be deported to a British colony; they were not permitted to see their relatives who lived in Palestine. The refugees decided to use passive resistance and had to be carried out forcibly onto two ships: the *New Zealand* and *Johann de Witt*. They had a Dutch crew and a British captain. On 26 December 1940, 1,580 refugees—849 men, 635 women and 96 children—arrived at the island of Mauritius in the Indian Ocean, then under British rule. They were taken to a former prison.

Men and women were put into separate compounds. Children were housed with women but, at the age of 13, boys were sent to live with the men. The refugees remained for five years in Mauritius and their situation became progressively better. They organized some cultural life, had their own newspaper *Camp News*, their own money, the *Substitute Shekel*, and received kosher food from the Jewish communities of South Africa and Australia. In 1942, some 200 young people were allowed to leave the camp in order to enlist in the Allied forces. After the war, the survivors were allowed to sail back to Haifa, where they arrived in August 1945 on board the *Franconia*. Left behind, in the small, well-tended Jewish cemetery of Mauritius, were the 124 people who had died during the years of exile.

MAURRAS, CHARLES

(1868–1952) Writer and antisemitic leader of the French extreme right-wing movement, Action Française.

Action Française was founded in 1898, three years after the Dreyfus Affair (in which a French Jewish colonel was falsely accused and imprisoned as a traitor). It was a group that expressed the antisemitic ideas that had fueled the Dreyfus Affair. Maurras was a leader of the intellectual right, and a well-known writer. Some have called him an outstanding original thinker. Others considered him a dangerous political fraud. He believed that the Greek and Roman cultures were the basis of European civilization, which had been corrupted by Judaism and Christianity.

In 1937, he was imprisoned for incitement to murder because of his aggressive verbal attacks on the Jewish prime minister of France, Léon BLUM. Later, he became a close friend of VICHY's first commissioner for Jewish affairs, Xavier VALLAT.

In 1944, during the postwar purge of Nazi collaborators, Maurras was tried. He was sentenced to life imprisonment for his pro-Vichy activities during the war.

MAUTHAUSEN

CONCENTRATION CAMP in Upper Austria, on the Danube river, near Linz. Intended at first (May 1938) to accommodate the overflow of prisoners from DACHAU, Mauthausen grew at such a pace that a cluster of smaller satellite camps were also established around it. The first was set up at nearby Gusen in

Forced labor along the "stairway to death" in Mauthausen

1940. Altogether, an estimated 200,000 prisoners were sent to Mauthausen and its sister camps; some 120,000 died there, including 38,000 Jews. It was used at first for common criminals and German political prisoners. Throughout the war it remained a camp primarily for political opponents of the Nazis or for persons considered dangerous to their regime.

Mauthausen was a FORCED LABOR camp. Conditions were so terrible that the death rate was among the highest of all the camps. The Nazis devised many forms of cruelty to kill the prisoners. They were made to carry heavy loads up 186 steps of a stone stairway, while on starvation rations. Crowded conditions and lack of sanitary facilities led to outbreaks of typhus and dysentery. Many prisoners did not survive more than a few days. Executions were carried out by phenol injections until a gas chamber was built in 1942. A crematorium was built to get rid of the bodies, but toward the end of the war its capacity became insufficient and a huge common grave was prepared.

The endless stream of prisoners came from all over occupied Europe. First Germans, then Republican Spaniards, who had fled to FRANCE after General Francisco Franco's victory in the Spanish Civil War, then a succession of Poles, Czechs and Russian prisoners of war, civilians from all over occupied western Europe and Yugoslav freedom fighters. Though a number of Jews had reached the camp with the others, the first all-Jewish contingent arrived in May 1941. It included hundreds of so-called "hostages" from Holland, followed by two other groups of Dutch Jews. Jews were singled out for the harshest treatment, and most of them died within a week of their arrival at the camp. In March 1945, an assembly camp for Jews was established at Gunskirchen. Plans were underway to kill all inmates at the time of the German surrender, but American troops reached and liberated Mauthausen in May 1945. The last commander of the camp, Franz Ziereis, who had tried to escape, was captured and shot.

MEDICAL EXPERIMENTS

Nazi doctors carried out a series of hideous medical experiments on some 7,000 prisoners—JEWS, GYPSIES, and prisoners of war—in CONCENTRATION CAMPS and DEATH CAMPS. Some experiments were for military purposes. Others were meant to prove Nazi racial theories (see RACISM). Established institutions in GERMANY, including the government, the NAZI PARTY, the medical services, and the army, worked together on these projects.

The military tests were supposed to determine the ability of human beings to survive under extreme conditions. Prisoners in DACHAU were made to drink salt water to measure their ability to adapt to harsh wartime conditions. They were exposed to high altitude pressure at 13 miles above the earth without an oxygen supply. Others were subjected to freezing temperatures. Many lost their lives as a result. Experiments carried out in RAVENSBRÜCK, left the victims permanently disabled or crippled. Prisoners were also given deadly diseases so they could become human guinea pigs to test out new vaccinations. At SACHSENHAUSEN experiments were performed in an effort to try to show that Gypsies had blood that was different from "Aryans." These experiments only succeeded in causing a great deal of suffering. Other experiments simulated war wounds and chemical warfare.

Often, the "research" was inspired by the perverted interest of the particular physician. The hideous atmosphere of the medical killing centers at AUSCHWITZ attracted mentally disturbed physicians like John Paul Kremer. His interest in the medical aspects of starvation were particularly cruel. No single doctor symbolized these terrible experiments more than Josef MENGELE. He conducted elaborate research at Auschwitz using extreme methods. Mengele was fascinated with the genetics of twins and dwarfs. He singled them out among the inmates for his cruel experiments and they lived and died under torture and terror. He also experimented to see if he could change eye color to conform to Nazi racial stereotypes. Dr. Carl Clauberg and Dr. Horst Schumann, also in Auschwitz, performed horrible experiments in sterilization. One thousand male and female prisoners were subjected to these experiments. One observer said that "Auschwitz was like a medical operation," with the doctors coordinating the killing process from beginning to end. All medical experiments had to be personally approved by Heinrich HIMMLER. The world has never seen such an outrageous violation of the oath taken by doctors to work for the good of their patients.

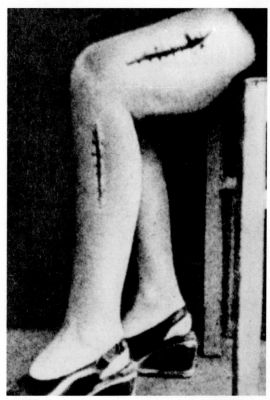

Picture of a woman's leg which had undergone experimentation in Ravensbrück

After the war, one of the TRIALS OF WAR CRIMINALS was devoted to doctors. The court determined that the experiments were meant to serve the goals of the Nazis and that none of them had any scientific value. Seven doctors were executed and nine received prison sentences.

MEIN KAMPF

("My Struggle")

Title of Adolf HITLER's book, which became the bible of the Nazi agenda. It was written in two volumes, later combined into one. The first volume is entitled *The Reckoning*, and the second *The National Socialist Movement*.

The Reckoning was written by Hitler while he was in prison, in 1924. He dictated it to Rudolf HESS, who would later become his deputy. The book focuses on ANTISEMITISM, power worship, the importance of racial purity and the uselessness of democracy. Hitler unveiled his plan for ARYAN world domination in this work.

> *The mightiest counterpart to the Aryan is represented by the Jew. In hardly any people in the world is the instinct of self-preservation developed more strongly than in the so-called "chosen"—of this, the mere fact of the survival of this race may be considered the best proof...*
>
> *Since the Jew—for reasons which will at once become apparent—was never in possession of a culture of his own, the foundations of his intellectual work were always provided by others...*
>
> *If the Jews were alone in this world they would stifle in filth and in garbage; they would try to get ahead of one another in a hate-filled struggle to exterminate one another...*
>
> From *Mein Kampf*

The style of the writing is stiff, heavy and repetitive. Even so, the book was a resounding success. By 1939, 5.2 million copies had been sold and the work had been translated into 11 languages. Nazis considered it an excellent wedding present for newly married couples.

The overall theme of the book is the racial superiority of the Aryan. It called for Germans to inject new strength into Germany after the embarrassing defeat they had suffered during World War I. According to *Mein Kampf*, the state should perform seven basic functions: place race at the center of its agenda, keep its race pure and clean, not allow weak and diseased people to have children, promote sports to the highest level, make the army the highest level of achievement for the young, teach the greatness of racial superiority, and awaken national pride and patriotism.

The Aryan race was, in Hitler's eyes, the chosen people—its superiority and its continued purity was essential. He divided the world into three groups: the founders, the bearers, and the destroyers of civilization and culture.

The first group, the founders of civilization and culture, were the Aryans. The second group were the morally subjugated societies, like the Japanese, and the third group, the destroyers, were the Jews.

According to Hitler's view, the Jews were the enemy of everything Aryan. The Aryan was a laborer linked to the land. The Jew was a parasite who never knew an honest day's labor. For Hitler, it was the Jews who had caused the defeat of Germany in World War I, and it was they who were responsible for the terrible situation in which Germany found itself as he was writing *Mein Kampf*.

The second volume of *Mein Kampf, The National Socialist Movement*, appeared in 1925. It is filled with clichés and attempts at philosophical analysis. While the first volume contains the semblance of a program, this volume lacks any serious organization.

MEMORIALS

see MUSEUMS AND MEMORIALS.

MENGELE, JOSEF

(1911–1979) German doctor who was chief physician at the AUSCHWITZ concentration camp from 1943 to 1944. He had full power to decide who would live and who would die in the camp: He sent an estimated 400,000 Jews that he considered "unfit for work" to the GAS CHAMBERS. He also initiated and conducted gruesome experiments on defenseless inmates, focusing on babies, dwarfs and twins. These experiments included forcible sterilization, amputations and injections of lethal substances to observe their reactions. His tests were painful, exhausting, often lethal, and traumatic for the CHILDREN who made up the bulk of his subjects. His objective was to "prove" the superiority of the ARYAN race.

Josef Mengele joined the Nazi Party in 1937, and entered the Waffen-SS Medical Corps in 1940. He rose swiftly through its ranks to become Hauptsturmführer in 1943. He remained in Auschwitz until the camp was evacuated in January 1945, and afterwards "disappeared." With the help of sympathizers, he managed to escape to South America after the war. He was granted political asylum in ARGENTINA in 1949. In 1959, nearly 15 years after the war, German authorities issued a warrant for his arrest, followed a year later by a request to Argentina for his extradition. Warned in time, he fled to Brazil, then to Paraguay. In 1985, the corpse of a Wolfgang

Gerhard, who had died in Brazil in a swimming accident in 1979, was identified by forensic specialists as Mengele's corpse.

M E R I N ,   M O S H E

(1906–1943) Chairman of the JUDENRAT (Jewish Council) in Eastern Upper SILESIA (a part of POLAND incorporated by the Germans into the Reich).

Before WORLD WAR II, Merin was a Zionist activist in the town of Sosnowiec. He became a member of the Sosnowiec's Jewish *Kehillah* (community association) in September 1939.

GERMANY invaded Poland on 1 September 1939 and Sosnowiec was occupied on 4 September. In January 1940, the Germans set up a Judenrat with Merin as its chairman. This Judenrat covered not only Sosnowiec but the entire region of eastern Upper Silesia. Merin was thus responsible for the welfare of about 100,000 Jews from 45 communities. Like other Judenrat chairmen, he was placed in the terrible position of having to provide for the needs of the Jewish population while at the same time obeying Nazi demands. With the help of the Jewish Police, Merin carefully obeyed German demands to have Jews from the entire region report for FORCED LABOR.

The Judenrat employed over 1,200 people and had many departments: police, health, welfare, education, soup kitchens, orphanages, archives, and others. Physical conditions for Jews in eastern Upper Silesia were somewhat better than in other parts of Poland. At first, these communities were not put into GHETTOS—unlike elsewhere in Poland.

In May 1942, the Nazis began DEPORTATIONS of the Jews to DEATH CAMPS. Merin followed German demands to have Jews report for deportation, believing he could save the rest. By August 1942, a third of the Jews in eastern Upper Silesia had been sent to AUSCHWITZ. Of those who were spared, many worked in factories that aided the German war effort. Merin believed that by keeping Jews working for the Nazis, he would be saving their lives.

Though Merin had support for his policies among many Jewish residents, there was much opposition—primarily from the Zionist YOUTH MOVEMENTS, who branded him a COLLABORATOR. Merin maintained that the Zionist youth movements, who were plan-

ning RESISTANCE activities, would risk the safety of the other Jews. In 1943, he turned over two Zionist activists to the Germans, and denounced members of a communist cell. A number of underground members, Zionist and communist, wanted to assassinate Merin.

Merin also tried to prevent Jews from making contacts with the Swiss, who were able to rescue some Jews by supplying them with South American passports. Despite his cooperation with the Germans, he was deported to his death in Auschwitz on 21 June 1943. The rest of the Jews of Eastern Upper Silesia followed soon after.

M   I   N   S   K

Capital of the Soviet Republic of BYELORUSSIA.

On the eve of the German invasion of SOVIET RUSSIA (22 June 1941), 90,000 JEWS lived in Minsk—a third of the city's total population. It was one of the first major cities in the Soviet Union to be occupied by the Germans. Very few Minsk Jews were able to flee to the Soviet interior and escape the Nazis. Thousands who tried to escape were stopped by German parachutists and forced to return.

The systematic persecution of the Jews soon began. The German army commander immediately established an internment camp for most of the city's male population. EINSATZGRUPPE B, a mobile killing unit went through the camp, rounding up and shooting the "Jews, criminals, functionaries, and Asiatics." On 8 July 1941, Einsatzgruppen and Byelorussian COLLABORATORS began to bring Jews to nearby woods and shoot them. In August, 5,000 Jews were killed by guns by the Einsatzgruppen.

On 20 July, the Germans issued an order to build a GHETTO. About 100,000 Jews from Minsk and nearby communities were forced to live in the small area. A FORCED LABOR camp with very harsh conditions was set up for Jews and SOVIET PRISONERS OF WAR.

A JUDENRAT (Jewish Council) was established, headed by Eliyahu (Ilya) Mushkin. A Jewish UNDERGROUND group, headed by Hersh Smolar, was also established. Mushkin, unlike a number of other Judenrat chairmen, cooperated with the Jewish underground. He even warned RESISTANCE leaders of approaching dangers. The main goals of the underground were rescue and resistance. Ghetto fighters escaped to the forests in order to join other fighting PARTISANS (the idea of armed resistance inside the ghetto was rejected). The Minsk underground also attempted to gather arms and set up an underground printing press, with the cooperation of the Judenrat. About 450 ghetto residents joined the underground, many of them young people. Mushkin made sure that some of what was produced in ghetto factories reached the partisans. A number of underground members, who worked in German military factories, sabotaged production.

On 7 November 1941, the Germans conducted an AKTION (killing operation) in the ghetto. They rounded up 12,000 Jews in the nearby Tuchinka forest, and machine gunned them into pits dug by the victims. A second Aktion occurred on 20 November, when the Germans murdered 7,000 more Jews in Tuchinka.

Following this, the Germans deported about 7,000 Jews from GERMANY to Minsk, and placed them in a separate ghetto. There was little contact between the main ghetto Russian Jews and the ghetto for German Jews. Within a year, over 35,000 Jews from Germany were deported to the Minsk ghetto,

and most of them were shot in Aktions that followed.

After the November killing operations, the Jewish underground stepped up its activities. It focused on planning escape routes to the forests. It appealed to the non-Jewish partisans to help ghetto residents escape to the forests. These appeals were useless since the local partisans offered little assistance. Jews who did join local Soviet partisan brigades were often victims of ANTISEMITISM by their partisan colleagues. This motivated Jewish fighters from Minsk to organize their own brigades.

A number of ghetto leaders who cooperated with the underground were captured by the Germans in 1942, including Ilya Mushkin. He was tortured and hanged one month later. His successor, Moshe Jaffe, also cooperated with the underground.

Minsk captured the attention of ss Chief Heinrich HIMMLER. When he arrived in Minsk, Himmler asked Einsatzgruppe B Chief Arthur Nebe to shoot a group of 100 people, so he could better visualize a "liquidation." After the shooting, Himmler expressed concern over the emotional effects of the shootings on German soldiers. Though shootings continued in Minsk, Himmler asked Nebe to come up

Humiliating Jews in Minsk, Soviet Russia

with other, cleaner killing methods—such as mobile gas vans (see GAS CHAMBERS, GAS VANS, AND CREMATORIA).

The Germans ordered another killing operation at the beginning of March 1942. They forced the Judenrat to hand over 5,000 unskilled Jews. In keeping with the wishes of the Jewish underground, the Judenrat refused. The Germans took revenge by ordering Judenrat members to dig a pit in a ravine at the ghetto's center. The Germans then ordered the director of the ghetto orphanage to bring its CHILDREN to the Judenrat building. When they passed by the newly dug pit, the children were thrown into it and burned alive. In addition to the children, the Nazis took revenge by shooting over 5,000 men, women, and children.

This atrocity led to an attempt to escape into the forests by about 10,000 Jews,many of whom lost their lives. The Jews from Minsk were active in establishing seven partisan units in the forests. Among them was the Zorin Unit, led by Minsk resistance activist Shalom Zorin. This unit provided protection in the forests to over 600 Jewish women and children.

The killings continued into the summer. During the last days of July 1942, the Germans and Byelorussian collaborators killed about 30,000 Jews in ditches outside the city.

Immediately before this Aktion, the Germans ordered Moshe Jaffe to lie to the ghetto population by telling them that everything would be all right. However, as Jews assembled in the town square, and in the presence of German trucks, Jaffe screamed out: "Jews, these bloody killers are lying to you—run for your lives!" Jaffe was then shot and killed by the Germans. Only 9,000 Jews were left in the ghetto by the end of the summer.

Atrocities continued into the following year. In September 1943, the Germans began the liquidation of the Minsk ghetto. On 21 October 1943, most of the ghetto's remaining 4,000 Jews were shot at the nearby village of Maly Trostinets. Others were killed in gas vans. The Soviets entered the city of Minsk on 3 July 1944, but except for a few Jews in hiding, none remained.

A memorial to the Jewish victims of the HOLOCAUST in Minsk was built immediately after the war. It is the only one in Soviet Russia to mention that the victims were Jews.

M I S C H L I N G E

Offspring of mixed marriages between Jews and non-Jews.

The NUREMBERG LAWS of September 1935 lay down serious restrictions on Jews but failed to define who was considered a Jew under the law. Therefore, on 14 November 1935, a precise formulation of who was a Jew was established according to Reich law.

A Jew was defined as a person with at least three grandparents who were full JEWS. A *Mischlinge* of the first degree was a person with two Jewish grandparents and a second-degree *Mischlinge* had one Jewish grandparent. A person would also be considered a Jew if he or she were a member of the Jewish religious community. These definitions reflect a compromise between the Nazis and the ministers of the REICHSTAG administration. The ministers wanted to define non-Aryans as persons with four Jewish grandparents, while the Nazis also wanted to consider half and quarter Jews as Jews. Estimates of the number of people affected range from 110,000 to 260,000.

Restrictions were applied to *Mischlinge*. Those of the first degree were barred from the army and high schools and could only marry other *Mischlinge* of the same status. Those of the second degree could serve in the army and marry Germans, but faced certain professional barriers and could not be members of the NAZI PARTY.

At various times the question of the treatment of the *Mischlinge* came up for discussion. Reinhard HEYDRICH called for sterilization, but medical tech-

> *The fact is that in deporting half-Jews, German blood is being sacrificed…. The half-Jew's intelligence and excellent education, linked to their ancestral German heritage, make them natural leaders outside of Germany…. I prefer to see half-Jews die a natural death inside Germany, although from three to four decades may be necessary to achieve this purpose*
>
> Wilhelm Stuckart, State Secretary in Germany's Ministry of the Interior

nique for a mass program of sterilization had not yet been perfected. The WANNSEE CONFERENCE failed to make decisions about *Mischlinge*. In April 1942, Adolf EICHMANN and his advisors argued for a special ghetto. Later that year, when SS experts reported that they now had the technical capacity to sterilize 72,700 first-degree *Mischlinge*, Eichmann recommended annulling all mixed marriages, deporting the Jewish partner and offering sterilization to the CHILDREN as a "gracious favor." Adolf HITLER, who took a close personal interest in the fate of the *Mischlinge*, did not agree.

In the end, since Nazi legal experts failed to deal with this grey area of racial definition, most of the *Mischlinge* survived the war.

MORGENTHAU, HENRY, JR.

(1891–1967) U.S. statesman. Born in New York, he was the son of U.S. statesman and one-time ambassador to Turkey, Henry Morgenthau, Sr.

Henry Morgenthau Jr. worked for the U.S. government in the areas of agriculture and economic affairs. A leading figure of President Franklin D. ROOSEVELT's "New Deal" team, he became secretary of the treasury in 1934, and worked to stabilize the economy. After WORLD WAR II broke out, he organized the Liaison Committee in the Treasury, which

We knew in Washington, from August 1942 on, that the Nazis were planning to exterminate all the Jews of Europe. Yet, for nearly 18 months after the first reports of the Nazi horror plan, the State Department did practically nothing. Officials dodged their grim responsibility, procrastinated when concrete rescue schemes were placed before them, and even suppressed information about atrocities in order to prevent an outraged public opinion from forcing their hand.... This gave us a front-row view of those 18 terrible months of inefficiency, buck-passing, bureaucratic delay and sometimes what appeared to be calculated obstructionism...these officials always preferred committees to action.... Lacking either the administrative drive or the emotional commitment, they could not bring about prompt United States action on behalf of the desperate people.

Henry Morgenthau, Jr.

Henry Morgenthau, Jr. (left) with President Franklin D. Roosevelt, 1941

helped the Allied Powers to hire U.S. firms for the manufacture of airplanes and munitions.

Beginning in August 1942, he became very concerned about the growing news of the murder of European Jews. He was extremely critical of the U.S. State Department for its reluctance to take any action to rescue the victims. Finally, late in 1943, he convinced the State Department to approve a proposal by the WORLD JEWISH CONGRESS to transfer private U.S. funds to Europe for the rescue of French and Romanian Jews. Morgenthau also worked with Roosevelt on the relocation of European REFUGEES. He was largely responsible for getting the President to establish the WAR REFUGEE BOARD in 1944.

After the war, he put forward the Morgenthau Plan, which proposed the conversion of GERMANY into mainly a farming area so that it could never again threaten the peace of Europe. The plan was considered for a brief time but was never adopted.

M O R O C C O

Country in North Africa. From 1912 to 1956, most of the country was governed by FRANCE and a small part by SPAIN. By 1939, there were about 200,000 JEWS living in Morocco, the largest Jewish community in North Africa.

In the 1930s, a campaign of antisemitic PROPA-GANDA was carried out by both Arab and French groups. In spite of this, thousands of Jewish REFUGEES came to Morocco in 1939 and 1940, as the war spread throughout central and eastern Europe and France. In the summer of 1940, when France was divided between the Nazi conquerors in the north and the pro-Nazi VICHY government in the south, most of the French administration in Morocco declared loyalty to Vichy.

The Moroccan ruler, King Muhammad, was sympathetic to the Jews. He declared that in his eyes they were equal to his other subjects. However, he had no power to make policy decisions. Between 1940 and 1942, the French government forced him to sign antisemitic decrees. In October 1940, the Vichy government in Morocco put into effect the Nazi racial laws that had already been passed in France. All Jews employed in government jobs were fired, and all Jewish students in state-owned schools were forced to leave. Only a tiny number of Jews were allowed to continue to work in the medical and legal professions. When food began to be rationed, Jews received only half of the rations given to the Arab population. In 1941, detention and FORCED LABOR CAMPS were established. Prisoners were held in the camps for political (not racial) reasons, but most of them were Jews. Among these

prisoners were many of the refugees who had escaped to Morocco in 1939 and 1940.

On 11 November 1942, the American army liberated Morocco and its Jews. However, it took months for all antisemitic rulings to be canceled and all prisoners of the detention camps liberated. A few weeks after the liberation, a local French antisemitic group organized violent demonstrations against Jews in the main cities.

MOSLEY, SIR OSWALD

(1896–1980) British Fascist leader. For a short period he served in the British Labor Government of 1929, but resigned that year to form his own party. His party failed to get even one seat in the next election.

Although Mosley claimed that he was not antisemitic, there were many references to "alien" power in his program and his party newsletter carried open attacks on JEWS. This trend was emphasized by the British Union of Fascists (BUF), which he founded in 1932. Like the Italian Fascists, his followers wore black shirts and marched to bands with flags flying. Concentrating their demonstrations and marches on densely Jewish neighborhoods, Mosley's Fascists became violent. Their physical attacks on Jews and Jewish property was similar to Nazi and Fascist ruffianism on the European continent. The frustrated commissioner of the London Police asked for the prohibition of "political" armies or at least the banning of uniforms. Such laws were introduced in 1937 after the so-called "Battle of Cable Street" in the East End of London, when Fascists on the one hand and Jews and anti-Fascists on the other came to serious blows. The BUF received little support in elections during the 1930s. After the outbreak of WORLD WAR II, the BUF was outlawed and Mosley was imprisoned from 1940 to 1943. In 1948, and again in the late 1950s, he tried to found new movements, but they never caught on.

MÜLLER, HEINRICH

(1900–?) ss general and chief of the GESTAPO. During World War I, Müller volunteered as a fighter pilot and received decorations for his bravery.

In 1919, Müller began to work for the Munich

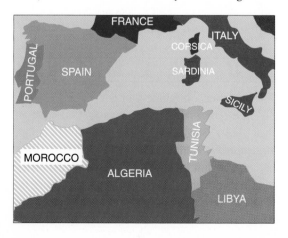

municipal police. When Reinhard HEYDRICH became the Bavarian police chief in 1933, Müller soon became one of his most trusted aides and a strong supporter of the Nazis. Müller joined the SS and the SD Security Service, but only became a member of the NAZI PARTY in 1939. He advanced quickly in the SS through complete loyalty to Heydrich, and reached the rank of SS lieutenant general.

When Heydrich moved from Munich to head the Gestapo office in Berlin, Müller moved with him in 1934. There he headed the department that investigated suspected opponents of the Nazi regime, including JEWS. From September 1939 until 1945, Müller was head of the Gestapo. He was, at the same time, deputy commander of the Security Police and the security service of the Nazi party (SD). Under Müller, the Gestapo expanded greatly and became the most feared police agency in Europe.

Müller was a central figure in carrying out the Holocaust. He was the commander of Adolf EICHMANN, who organized the DEPORTATIONS of Jews to the DEATH CAMPS in occupied POLAND. Müller himself personally authorized deportations and executions. He represented the Gestapo at the WANNSEE CONFERENCE in BERLIN on 20 January 1942. It was there that the

plan for the "FINAL SOLUTION" was decided.

In June 1942, Müller ordered that all traces of mass murder carried out by the mobile killing units (EINSATZGRUPPEN) in eastern Europe and at the death camps in occupied Poland be removed. Special groups of prisoners were forced to reopen mass graves and burn the bodies (see AKTION 1005).

Müller served the Nazis faithfully until the collapse of the THIRD REICH in 1945. He was last seen at Hitler's command bunker during the Soviet attack on Berlin in April–May 1945. Müller disappeared in the last days of the war. His fate is not absolutely known.

MUNICH AGREEMENT

Agreement between GERMANY, GREAT BRITAIN, FRANCE and ITALY signed at Munich by the leaders of these countries on 29 September 1938. Adolf HITLER had launched his demand for the Sudeten region of CZECHOSLOVAKIA. British premier Neville Chamberlain flew twice to Germany to try to dissuade him. Hitler only extended his demands and so the western powers mobilized for war. However, Chamberlain—architect of the policy of "appeasement" (making concessions to Hitler in the hope that he would make no further demands)—suggested a further conference, with the participation of the French leader, Eduard Daladier and the Italian dictator, Benito MUSSOLINI. This was held at Munich and Hitler's demands were accepted. In return Hitler promised a policy of peace ("this is peace in our time" announced Chamberlain). However, a few months later—in March 1939—he broke his word and invaded the rest of Czechoslovakia. This led Britain and France to adopt a policy of resistance to aggression instead of appeasement.

MUSELMANN

A German term meaning "Muslim." It was used to describe CONCENTRATION CAMP inmates who were in their last stages of physical deterioration. *Muselmänner* (plural) had almost no flesh on their bodies, a hollow look in their eyes and could barely remain standing on their feet. Since they were no longer of use to the Nazis as workers, and could not endure the harshness of camp life, they had no

Heinrich Müller (left) seated next to high officers

hope of survival. Although the origin of the usage of the word is unknown, it has been related to the image of a Muslim kneeling low to pray.

MUSEUMS AND MEMORIALS

HOLOCAUST memorials attempt to combine the recollection of history with tribute to the memory of those who died. Even before the end of WORLD WAR II, memorials to the victims of the Holocaust were established. As the invading Russian army liberated eastern Poland, DEATH CAMPS were discovered. In late 1944, MAJDANEK outside of LUBLIN, POLAND, was turned into one of the first Holocaust memorials. The camp's many barracks house the museum and memorial to those who had been murdered there. A huge mound of ashes, from hundreds of thousands of cremated bodies, is found at this memorial.

In the spring of 1945, Nathan Rapaport unveiled his large sculpture in tribute to the WARSAW ghetto fighters (see WARSAW GHETTO UPRISING). It is a two-sided, 36-foot bronze monument built in the center of the former Warsaw GHETTO. On the front face of the sculpture, Rapaport depicts the fighters under the leadership of Mordechai ANIELEWICZ. On the back, he shows a DEATH MARCH. The bronze statue is mounted on a black granite wall, the very granite that Adolf HITLER had imported from Sweden for his proposed victory monument. A replica of this memorial stands at YAD VASHEM, in Jerusalem.

In 1947, the Polish government established a memorial at the notorious AUSCHWITZ-Birkenau death camp. Auschwitz I is a museum contained in a series of barracks. Each one has a different display focusing on the prisoners and camp life. At Birkenau a memorial stands with inscriptions in the many languages of the victims. Monuments were set up on the sites of other major camps and killing sites throughout Europe.

As survivors returned to their home towns in search of family members and friends, they began to build memorials to those people who had been murdered. These memorials took many forms, from simple plaques to statues and depictions of heroism.

Communist countries erected large sculptures as memorials to the victims of FASCISM. Often, these memorials did not mention that the victims were Jewish. For example, this was true for the memorial at BABI YAR, where most of the victims were Jews. This was only changed after the fall of communism.

In 1949, Kibbutz Lohamei Ha-Gettaot, the kibbutz founded by former ghetto RESISTANCE fighters, established the GHETTO FIGHTERS' HOUSE, to which they have added a CHILDREN's museum. The State of ISRAEL memorialized the Holocaust in Yad Vashem, which has a CHILDREN's memorial and a Valley of the Lost Communities.

In the 1970s and early 1980s, many memorials were built. In 1977, the SIMON WIESENTHAL CENTER was created in Los Angeles. In 1980, the United States Congress voted to build a national memorial for the Holocaust on the Washington Mall, and this, the UNITED STATES HOLOCAUST MEMORIAL MUSEUM, was opened in 1993. Holocaust memorials have been created in many large cities in Northern America and Europe.

Monument on the site of Plaszów camp

(left top) Memorial at the site of 18 Mila Street, headquarters of the Jewish Fighting Organization in the Warsaw Ghetto Uprising; (right top) Memorial to Hungarian victims who died at Mauthausen. The inscription reads "Never Forget"; (left bottom) Monument at the entrance to the site of the Majdanek camp; (right bottom) Part of the monument in the Birkenau camp—the inscription is in many languages

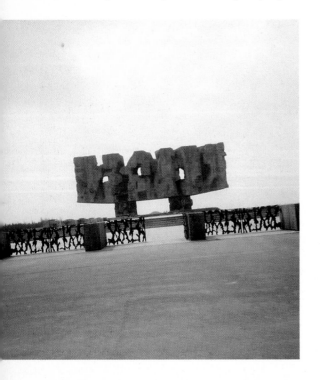

(left top) Memorial on site of the crematoria in Dora camp; (right top) Memorial at the site of the Treblinka death site. On each stone is carved the name of a community which suffered or was destroyed in the Holocaust; (bottom) Monument in Majdanek death camp built over a pile of ashes of the victims

MUSIC OF THE HOLOCAUST

Music related to the HOLOCAUST is linked by a common theme of oppression, either of the individual or of an entire people. It has a wide variety of styles and forms. Some of the earliest expressions in music of Nazi persecution were the creations of German communists and socialists who had been sent to CONCENTRATION CAMPS as political prisoners. Best known from this prewar period is the song "Die Moorsoldaten" (The peat-bog soldiers). The words of the song describe the harsh life and secret hopes of the imprisoned laborers.

The government of Adolf HITLER did not tolerate modern art in any form in GERMANY. Nazi racial decrees banned public performance of music by Jewish composers and forced Jewish musicians from their jobs. Many important composers who were not Jews chose to leave the country. Others remained and either cooperated with the Nazis or chose "internal exile"—refusing to publish or perform their works while the Nazis were in power. Jewish musicians who remained in Germany were segregated into all-Jewish performance societies (KULTURBUND DEUTSCHER JUDEN). The Nazis finally dissolved these in 1941.

Music continued to be created and performed during the war, in the GHETTOS, concentration camps, and partisan hideouts of Nazi-occupied Europe. In the field of classical music, there was much musical activity in the Czech concentration camp of THERESIENSTADT (Terezin). There the Germans permitted—for PROPAGANDA purposes—recitals of chamber music, opera, and even the creation of new works. Music-making took place in varying ways in all the ghettos and CAMPS. Sometimes, this was with Nazi approval. Ghetto orchestras were set up to employ and distract the residents. In the concentration and DEATH CAMPS music performed by official camp orchestras accompanied prisoners as they marched to and from work. It also served the terrible purpose of drowning out the sounds of executions. Camp orchestras were staffed by prisoners whose lives had been spared, if only temporarily, due to their musical talents. Sometimes, the music was made in secret, as with the countless songs that circulated among the prisoners. These songs shed much light on the day-to-day lives of the victims of Nazism. Their words refer to hunger, smuggling, ghetto personalities, hidden CHILDREN, DEPORTATIONS, and death. Music also played an important role in boosting the morale of the Jewish PARTISANS, the UNDERGROUND, and anti-Nazi RESISTANCE fighters.

Music-making played an important role among non-Jewish victims of Nazi persecution: GYPSIES, Polish and SOVIET PRISONERS OF WAR, and religious groups (such as the Jehovah's Witnesses). Hundreds of songs relating to the experiences of prisoners in more than 30 Nazi concentration camps were collected by the Polish ex-prisoner Alexander Kulisiewicz. They now form part of the archives of the UNITED STATES HOLOCAUST MEMORIAL MUSEUM in Washington, D.C.

The Holocaust was the subject of a number of outstanding compositions. By 1941, the British composer Michael Tippett wrote the oratorio *A Child of our Time* based on the story of Herschel GRYNSZPAN. Among many important works from the postwar period are: *A Survivor from Warsaw* by Arnold Schoenberg (1948), the *Symphony no. 13* ("Babi Yar") by Dmitri Shostakovich (1962), and *Different Trains* by Steve Reich (1988). The number of musical pieces inspired by the Holocaust continues to grow each year.

MUSSERT, ANTON ADRIAAN

(1894–1946) Dutch Fascist (see FASCISM AND FASCIST MOVEMENTS) and COLLABORATOR. He founded the National Socialist movement in Holland (the NETHERLANDS) in 1931.

Mussert was an engineer by trade. He was not originally antisemitic and his politics were influenced more by economics and nationalism than by hatred of Jews. Following the rise of Nazi GERMANY and the events of KRISTALLNACHT, he came up with his own solution to the "Jewish problem." He called for a Jewish national homeland to be set up in the sparsely settled territories of Dutch, French and British Guyana on the northeastern coast of South America. When the Germans took over the Netherlands, Mussert promoted a "federation of Nordic nations," which would include the Netherlands. In 1942, the Germans allowed him to call himself "Leader of the Dutch People," but he did not have any real power. He did try to help some JEWS, but with little success. When Germany was defeated and the Netherlands liberated, Mussert was arrested for treason and collaboration with the enemy. He was sentenced to death and executed.

MUSSOLINI, BENITO

(1883–1945) Italian dictator, founder of FASCISM. Originally a socialist, he broke away from socialism and in 1919 founded his own party based on a program of nationalism and anti-communism. In 1922, he and his followers marched on Rome, the Italian capital, and seized power.

In 1925, Mussolini, who by now called himself *Il Duce* (The Leader), became ITALY's dictator. Although he had from time to time made anti-Jewish statements, he rejected ANTISEMITISM. In fact, JEWS were among the founders of Fascism and were active in the party. Mussolini said in 1932, "I have no love for the Jews but they have great influence everywhere and it is better to leave them alone." He did not attempt to create a "Jewish Problem" until he became politically joined with Adolf HITLER. In 1935, he attacked Ethiopia, which alienated him from the other European countries and drove him to form an alliance—the "Axis"—with Hitler. He also joined Hitler in supporting General Franco in the Spanish Civil War (1936–1939).

In 1938, departing from his former views, he began to adopt a policy of antisemitism. A series of decrees forbade Jews to teach, banned mixed marriages, and expelled foreign Jews (the last measure was canceled under pressure from the United States). These and other measures came entirely from Mussolini and there is no evidence that he was under any pressure from Hitler. Mussolini entered WORLD WAR II as Hitler's junior partner in spring 1940, when he launched a blundering attack on GREECE (from which he had to be extricated by German troops). This was the signal for more anti-Jewish measures, although he refused to imitate the harshness of German anti-Jewish policies. He even acted kindly toward Jews in those areas that were conquered by Italy. However, in 1943, he was overthrown and imprisoned by his own Fascist Grand Council, which felt the time had come to make peace with the Allies.

He was rescued by the Germans, who kept him on as the puppet head of the part of Italy they controlled, but he no longer made policy and was irrelevant for the rest of the war. Mussolini had no say in the German attempts to impose the "FINAL SOLUTION" in north and central Italy. At the end of the war, Mussolini was executed by Italian PARTISANS.

Benito Mussolini (second from the left) exercising with his soldiers

n

NACHT UND NEBEL

see NIGHT AND FOG.

NATIONAL SOCIALIST GERMAN WORKERS' PARTY (NSDAP)

see NAZI PARTY.

NATZWEILER-STRUTHOF

German CONCENTRATION CAMP.

The camp was established by the Germans in 1940 in French territory that was annexed by GERMANY. It was located in the Alsace region of FRANCE and was one of the smaller concentration camps. Its location was chosen because of the nearby granite quarries. Granite was mined by prisoners for German construction projects.

The first prisoners arrived in May 1941 and built the camp. It was opened in the summer of 1942. By 1944, 7,000 to 8,000 prisoners were held in Natzweiler, the main camp. Prisoners worked on construction projects, in the maintenance of the camp, and later in the production of German armaments. Beginning in the summer of 1943, captured members of the RESISTANCE in western Europe were sent to Natzweiler as the Germans tried to put down resistance activity. These prisoners became known as NIGHT AND FOG prisoners. After they were arrested, they disappeared. A large subcamp system with over 20,000 prisoners was also established in 1944 around Natzweiler-Struthof.

An experimental GAS CHAMBER was built in the summer of 1943 in Natzweiler. Jewish and GYPSY prisoners were selected for pseudo-scientific MEDICAL EXPERIMENTS. Some of these experiments involved the use of poison gas. Over 80 bodies of gassed prisoners were sent for study to the Strasbourg University Institute of Anatomy.

Natzweiler-Struthof was evacuated in September 1944, as the Allied forces approached. The subcamp

The Natzweiler-Struthof concentration camp

system was emptied in March 1945. Prisoners were forced on DEATH MARCHES to DACHAU concentration camp in southern Germany. More than 17,000 prisoners died in the Natzweiler-Struthof camp system. The site is kept as a memorial with a cemetery and a monument.

NAZI PARTY (NSDAP)

("National Socialist German Workers' Party")

Political party that ruled GERMANY from 1933 to 1945. The Nazi Party was founded on 5 January 1919. It rose to power from humble beginnings in a little more than a decade.

From the beginning, ANTISEMITISM was a major point of its platform. Anton Drexler, a locksmith by trade, was its founder. He never succeeded in recruiting more than 40 members.

Adolf HITLER's involvement in the party came about by accident early on. In September 1919, he received orders from the German army's Political Department to investigate the new party. He was won over by the Nazis and recruited to become a member. Party members recognized Hitler as a powerful public speaker, and chose him for party leadership. Along with Dietrich Eckart and Ernst RÖHM, Hitler began attracting larger and larger audiences to party meetings. Röhm and his associates provided the power by which the Nazis intimidated opponents and broke up their meetings. Hitler excelled in the party's PROPAGANDA efforts. By 1920, party meetings were drawing thousands. It was at one of these meetings that Hitler first declared the 25 points of the party platform. This "unalterable" program hinted at the degradation and expulsion of the Jews, the cancellation of the Versailles Treaty (see glossary), and the permission given to Germans living outside Germany to return to their country of origin. All of this came to pass when the Nazis came to power.

Following the failure of the Beer Hall Putsch (see glossary) on 9 November 1923, Hitler was sent to prison and the party was banned. However, following his release, the party was reestablished on 27 February 1925. The Nazi Party remained in existence until it was declared illegal by the Allies after Germany was defeated in 1945.

The Nazis' popularity with the German people increased steadily between 1924 and 1932. In the 1928 elections, the party received only 3 percent of the votes. By 1932 they had 37 percent of the seats. Finally, in the elections of 1933, Hitler and the Nazis won 43.9 percent of the popular vote. Since they were now the largest party, the Nazis formed the government. By the end of the war, membership in the Nazi Party had reached 8.5 million.

When in power, Nazi Party leadership was organized into 18 *Reichsleiter* (state leaders) who held the important ministerial posts. There were 32

Nazi Party rally, 1931

Meeting of the NSDAP, Frankfurt, 1932

Gauleiter (district heads) who were party representatives in different territories. Above all, the party looked to the undisputed, central leadership of its FÜHRER (leader), Adolf Hitler. His word was law.

The Nazi Party developed a broad network of organizations, which further extended its power. They included the SA Stormtroopers, the SS, the SD, the the HITLER YOUTH, and various labor unions.

NAZI PROPAGANDA

see PROPAGANDA, NAZI.

NAZI-SOVIET PACT

Non-aggression pact between Nazi GERMANY and the SOVIET UNION. It was signed on 23 August 1939 by both countries' foreign ministers, Joachim von RIBBENTROP and Vyacheslav Molotov (hence it was also known as the Ribbentrop-Molotov Pact). The pact shocked the world because until then, the two countries had been the bitterest of enemies. BRITAIN and FRANCE had been counting on Russian support in the event of a war, and had been negotiating an alliance with the Soviet Union.

The pact was the result of tactical and practical considerations on both sides. The Russian ruler, Joseph STALIN, felt let down by the Allies' (France and Britain) policy of APPEASEMENT and no longer believed that these countries were determined to fight Adolf HITLER. Stalin also realized that he would need time to prepare Russia for war should it become necessary. At the same time, he was not opposed to enlarging his country's sphere of influence. A number of secret protocols allotted FINLAND, ESTONIA and LATVIA to the Russian sphere of influence and Lithuania to Germany's. POLAND was divided between the two powers—Stalin stated his country's "interest" in Bessarabia. Germany, though bitterly opposed to Bolshevism, was anxious to prevent an agreement between the Soviet Union and the Allies. Hitler secretly planned to defeat first the Western powers and then turn his attention to conquering Russia. The Nazi-Soviet Pact, which covered an initial 10-year period, stated that both countries wanted peace between them.

A week after the signing of the pact, Germany invaded Poland. The pact lasted less than two years. Hitler's hatred for communism, his need for raw materials and Germany's obsession for LEBENSRAUM

Soviet foreign minister Vyacheslav Molotov signing the Nazi-Soviet Pact, 14 August 1939. Behind him (in dark suit) German foreign minister Joachim von Ribbentrop and (in white suit) Joseph Stalin

("living space") led Hitler to prepare to invade the Soviet Union as early as the winter of 1940. Germany launched its attack on Russia on 22 June 1941.

NEO-NAZISM

"Neo" means "new." The term "Neo-Nazis" refers to

The cartoonist Low reacts to the Nazi-Soviet Pact in which two deadly enemies suddenly announced their friendship

parties, groups, and individuals who since the end of WORLD WAR II have accepted the racist, antisemitic, and political ideas of Adolf HITLER and his NAZI PARTY. Although the Nazis were defeated, the horrors of the Holocaust exposed, and Nazism condemned, these hateful ideas still have followers. Supporters of these groups also believe in HOLOCAUST DENIAL.

The central ideas of Neo-Nazism are a belief in white supremacy (that whites are superior to all other people), a hatred of JEWS and blacks, and an admiration for Hitler. Followers do not look only to the past—to Nazi GERMANY. Neo-Nazism also has a role in the politics of today. For example, there are Neo-Nazi skinheads around the world. They not only proudly wear Nazi symbols, but have developed their own music, culture, and dress. Skinheads have committed many racist and antisemitic attacks and murders over the last decade. They are seen by many older leaders of white supremacist groups as "shock troops."

In Germany, parties that openly support ANTISEMITISM, fly the SWASTIKA, and identify with Nazi achievements have been outlawed. However, there are still groups there that continued such programs. Neo-Nazism gained some support in LATIN AMERICA in the postwar years, although it later declined.

Even in the United States and CANADA there are skinheads and other groups who are Neo-Nazis in name or in fact. For example, a group that calls itself the National Alliance is led by a Neo-Nazi William Pierce, who has glorified Hitler. His writings are read by many white supremacists. He was the favorite writer of Timothy McVeigh, charged with the 1995 Oklahoma City bombing, which killed 167 people. There is also a school of religious thought called Christian Identity which believes that whites ("Aryans") are God's "chosen people." It further believes that Jews are the actual offspring of the devil, and that minorities—whom they call "mud people"—are not even human beings. These beliefs have been adopted by many Neo-Nazis, including the Aryan Nations group located in Idaho. In Germany, as in other countries, Neo-Nazi groups remain on the fringe—banned in many places. At the same time, the very fact that they continue to exist is a cause for concern. This is especially true since Hitler's Nazi Party also started as a small fringe group.

NETHERLANDS, THE

Country in western Europe (also known as Holland). It was invaded by the German army on 10 May 1940 and surrendered on 14 May. Its queen, Wilhelmina, and the government fled the country for England.

Dutch Jews being deported to Westerbork transit camp from where they were sent to death camps in eastern Europe

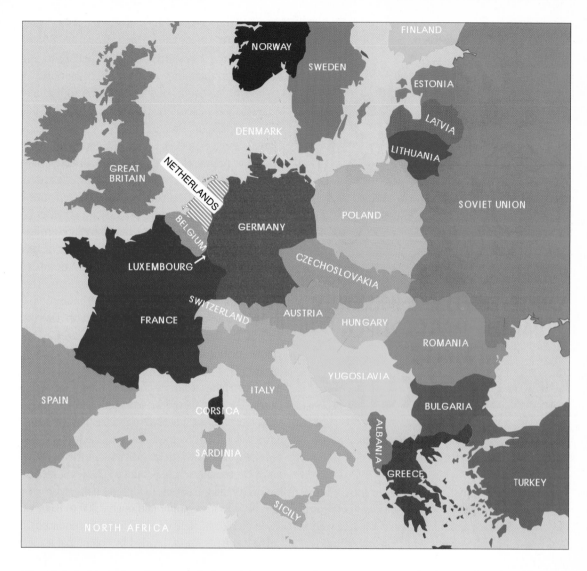

They left behind the directors of the ministries, who then functioned as a kind of substitute government. A civil administration, headed by the German representative, Arthur SEYSS-INQUART, was soon established according to a personal order of Adolf HITLER. This showed Hitler's desire to combine the Dutch (the people of the Netherlands) with the "Greater Germanic Community," since he considered the Dutch to be a "strayed" Germanic tribe.

Just after the Nazi occupation, the Dutch Jewish community numbered about 140,000. About 75,000 of them lived in the capital, Amsterdam. Most were Dutch citizens, whose ancestors had settled in the country in the beginning of the seventeenth century. Over 15,000 were refugees who had fled Germany after Hitler rose to power. During the war,

about 107,000 JEWS were deported to death and CONCENTRATION CAMPS—mainly to AUSCHWITZ (60,026) and SOBIBÓR (34,313). Of these, about 5,200 survived.

Nazi anti-Jewish policies in the Netherlands were the most extreme in western Europe. This was largely because of the intensity of the Nazi grip on the country. The leadership in Holland was a team of devoted, extremely antisemitic—mostly Austrian—Nazis. It was helped by a smoothly run and cooperative Dutch administration.

The long and harsh series of anti-Jewish measures started in the fall of 1940. In November 1940, ARYANIZATION began, and all Jews were required to register their businesses, and then themselves. In February, a *Joodsche Raad* (Jewish Council see JUDENRAT) was established by the Germans. A brutal

YANKEE - ENGELSMAN - BOLSJEWIEK DANSEN NAAR DE PIJPEN VAN DE

JODENKLIEK

"Yankee, Englishman and Bolshevik all dance to the Jewish tune" — Nazi poster in Dutch

round-up of 389 Jewish young people took place. This was Nazi revenge for a minor incident between German policemen and the owner of a Jewish cafe. The young people were sent to concentration camps; only one survived.

Throughout 1941, laws were passed that isolated Jews from the rest of society. These included banning Jews from public buildings and recreation sites, night curfews, limiting shopping to 3:00–5:00 p.m., a ban on the use of public transportation, the removal of all Jewish CHILDREN from public and private schools and universities, and the establishment of a separate Jewish school system. After late 1941, LABOR CAMPS were opened and the Germans began to send Jews to them to work at FORCED LABOR. Jews were removed from many parts of the country and concentrated in a limited number of places. Beginning in May 1942, Jews were forced to wear the yellow BADGE. By April 1943, Jews were allowed to live only in Amsterdam or the Vught concentration camp, and by 29 September 1943, all Jews had been removed from their homes. DEPORTATIONS began in mid-July 1942. Jews were arrested or rounded-up, and deported to WESTERBORK, the "Jewish transit camp." From there they were sent to DEATH CAMPS.

The attitude of the Dutch population to the persecutions was mixed. The positive reputation of the Dutch population, created mainly by Anne FRANK's diary, is exaggerated. A Dutch Nazi Movement had existed in prewar Holland, but it had attracted only a minor part of the population. However, the arrival of refugees from Germany in the 1930s led to increasing resentment toward Jews. Sharp criticism of anti-Jewish measures came from university professors and especially students. The universities of Leiden and Delft were (temporarily) closed down by the authorities because of strikes by students. The well-known "February Strike" (25–26 February 1941) in Amsterdam was sparked by anti-Jewish laws as well as by the declining economic situation. This unique demonstration of solidarity with the Jews, however, led the Nazis to increase their anti-Jewish policies. There were no further protests by the Dutch. The removal of Jews from schools and universities met with considerable resistance, but this resistance was broken by the Germans. Dutch police cooperated with the Nazis in carrying out the deportations. On the other hand, about 25,000 Jews, including 4,500 children, were hidden by non-Jewish citizens all over the country (although 7,000 to 8,000 of those "in hiding" were detected and/or denounced).

The *Joodsche Raad*, headed by communal leader Abraham Asscher and historian Professor David Cohen, developed many activities to sustain Jewish life. However, its policy of cooperating with the Germans caused much criticism and animosity, both at that time and after the war. A postwar Jewish "honorary court" even tried Asscher and Cohen and removed them from any communal position. No organized Jewish resistance activities were developed in Holland, but Jews were involved in general resistance activities.

NEURATH, CONSTANTIN, BARON VON

(1873–1956) German diplomat. He became foreign minister in 1932, and continued in that position after Adolf HITLER came to power the following year.

Baron von Neurath (right) standing next to Hitler

He supported Hitler's foreign policy and led the negotiations that brought about the alliance of Germany and Italy. He was replaced by Joachim von RIBBENTROP in February 1938. After that, von Neurath served as Reich Protector of BOHEMIA AND MORAVIA (1939–1941). As such, he was in charge of that country when repressive measures were carried out against political parties and against Jews. However, when these measures intensified, he was replaced by Reinhard HEYDRICH. Von Neurath was tried at Nuremberg (SEE TRIALS OF WAR CRIMINALS) for war crimes, crimes against peace and crimes against humanity, and sentenced to 15 years' imprisonment. He was released because of illness after serving eight years.

NIEMÖLLER, MARTIN

(1892–1984) German anti-Nazi pastor. He was a heroic World War I submarine commander who became a leading Protestant pastor in the anti-Nazi Confessing Church.

> *First they came for the communists, and I did not speak out because I was not a communist. Then they came for the trade unionists, and I did not speak out because I was not a trade unionist. Then they came for the Jews, and I did not speak out because I was not a Jew. Then they came for me, and there was no one left to speak for me.*
>
> *Reported statement by Martin Niemöller*

Since he was opposed to the pre-Nazi WEIMAR REPUBLIC, he at first welcomed the Nazi regime. By 1934, he recognized his error and formed the Pastors' Emergency League. In 1937, he came to lead the anti-Nazi Confessing Church. He was arrested, received a modest fine and freed. Then Adolf HITLER personally ordered him rearrested. He spent seven years in the SACHSENHAUSEN and DACHAU CONCENTRATION CAMPS, much of them in solitary confinement.

Freed in 1945, he organized the Stuttgart Confes-

Martin Niemöller

sion of Guilt, which declared the collective guilt of the German people for the war and their crimes. After the war, he again supported unpopular ideas calling for pacifism and a disarmed, neutral, unified GERMANY.

NIGHT AND FOG

("*Nacht und Nebel*")

German term for political prisoners from western Europe who disappeared without leaving a trace. In late 1941, Adolf HITLER issued an order that was signed by General Wilhelm KEITEL. It stated that UNDERGROUND activities directed against the Reich or the German occupation would be punished by the most severe measures. As a result, many thousands of civilians in western Europe were arrested and deported to GERMANY. There they were either quickly sentenced to death by special German courts and executed, or put into a camp. Nobody knew their fate. As the end of the war approached, any of these prisoners who remained alive shared the fate of the rest of the CONCENTRATION CAMP inmates. Only a small number survived.

NIGHT OF THE LONG KNIVES

see ROHM, ERNST; SA.

NISKO AND LUBLIN PLAN

Plan developed by the German government in the early months of WORLD WAR II. The Nisko and Lublin Plan aimed to resettle large numbers of Jews who had come under Nazi rule after the invasion of POLAND. According to this plan, JEWS were to be moved to a transit camp at Nisko, in the area of LUBLIN near the eastern Galician border. From there they would be sent to the Lublin district, which would become a "Jewish state under German administration." This idea was accepted in ss circles between September 1939 and March 1940. At that point, Adolf HITLER seemed to lose interest in territorial solutions for the Jews.

Adolf EICHMANN and his superior, Franz Stahlecker, were the chief designers of the Nisko and Lublin Plan. By September 1939, they began developing ideas for relocating the Jews who had come under German rule. In October, Eichmann began organizing a model transportation plan. Under his supervision, DEPORTATIONS were arranged from SILESIA, AUSTRIA, and BOHEMIA. Jews were told that they were being given an opportunity to create a new settlement in Poland. The GESTAPO obtained the voluntary participation of Jewish carpenters, engineers, and workers. Food and building materials were supplied by Jewish businesses.

The Jews arrived in Nisko in freight cars that had been sealed. When they reached the station, engineers, doctors, and builders were instructed to leave the trains. As they looked out over the empty, marshy fields to which they had been brought, Eichmann told them, "There are no apartments and no houses—if you will build your homes you will have a roof over your heads...if you dig for water, you'll have water." The skilled workers were then put to work.

Eichmann probably assumed that the 18 October transports were the beginning of a continuous process that he would oversee. However, the next day, Gestapo Chief Heinrich MÜLLER wired Eichmann that all deportations to Poland would require direct orders from BERLIN. One further transport did take place on 27 October. By the spring of 1940, the camp was closed.

There are a number of explanations for why the plan was halted. Eichmann blamed Hans FRANK, the governor general of Poland. Others have said there was local opposition to the arrival of masses of Jews. Heinrich HIMMLER mentioned difficulties in finding jobs and housing. In the end, the decision not to pursue the Nisko and Lublin Plan must be traced to Hitler's lack of interest. Hitler had no wish to give up space in his newly occupied territories for Jews. Even at this early stage in the war against the Jews, he may well have been thinking of another solution—a "FINAL SOLUTION"—to what he called the "Jewish problem."

NORWAY

Scandinavian country. When WORLD WAR II began there were an estimated 1,900 JEWS in Norway, including some 300 refugees from Central Europe. More than 1,000 lived in the capital, Oslo, and some 300 in Trondheim. There was little or no anti-

> *Jews are being punished because of their racial background, wholly and solely because they are Jews. According to God's Word, all people have the same human worth and the same human rights. Our state authorities are by law obliged to respect this basic view. To remain silent about this legalized injustice against the Jews would render ourselves co-guilty in this injustice.*
>
> From a 1943 statement by Lutheran bishops in Norway, read twice from all pulpits and published as the Church's New Year's message

semitism and the fascist National Unity Party (Nasjonal Samling), set up by Vidkun QUISLING, never received more than 2.5 percent of the vote.

Germany invaded Norway in April 1940. The royal family fled to London and set up a GOVERNMENT-IN-EXILE. The Germans appointed a commissar and though no formal laws were passed, the commissar began discriminatory measures against the Jews and their property. From 1 March 1942, Jewish identity papers bore the stamp for "Jew." The assassination of one of Quisling's bodyguards on 23 October 1942, was the excuse for mass arrests and DEPORTATIONS as well as the taking of Jewish property. This led to a vigorous reaction by the people of Norway and the Christian leaders. On 13 December 1942, an official protest was read by clergy in all religious establishments. It was no use. Of the 763 Jews that were deported, 739 of them died in the camps—410 men, 268 women and 61 children under 15. The Norwegian underground helped 900 Jews escape to SWEDEN. At the end of the war, there were no more Jews in Norway, but subsequently those who had escaped returned.

N O V Á K Y

Largest of the three FORCED LABOR CAMPS set up in central SLOVAKIA. One thousand six hundred Jews were sent there. The camp housed mostly skilled workers and carpenters and their families. It was managed by a JUDENRAT (Jewish Council), and was unusually well run. Facilities were generally good. Adequate medical care, makeshift schools for children, and a wide range of cultural and religious activities made this camp very different from the others. Its main problem was overcrowding, since many Jews tried to be sent to this place of comparative safety.

British commando unit boarding German prisoners of war captured in Norway

The Nováky camp was liberated in August 1944, at the time of the great national Slovak revolt. More than 200 men from the camp joined in the uprising. Nearly a fifth of them died fighting the Germans.

NOVEMBER POGROM

see KRISTALLNACHT.

NUREMBERG LAWS

Two racial laws passed in Nuremberg at a special session of the German parliament, the REICHSTAG, on 15 September 1935. They began a process of making RACISM an official part of German law. During the next eight years, thirteen other supplementary decrees were made.

The two laws passed in Nuremberg were the "Law Respecting Reich Citizenship" and the "Law for the Protection of German Blood and German Honor." The first said that only ARYANS (i.e., people with German blood) could be Reich citizens. Only Aryans had full political rights. JEWS became "state subjects," a lesser status that placed them under state

> "[The Nuremberg Laws are a] signal victory for the violent anti-Jewish wing of the Nazi Party."
>
> New York Herald Tribune, 16 September 1935, in an article entitled "The Shame of Nuremberg"
>
> "Nothing like the complete disinheritance and segregation of Jewish citizens...has been heard of since medieval times."
>
> The London Times, 17 September 1935
>
> "German policy is clearly to eliminate the Jew from German life.... Mortality and emigration provide the means."
>
> Eric Mills, British Commissioner for Migration and Statistics in Palestine, Foreign Office Papers, 6 October 1935

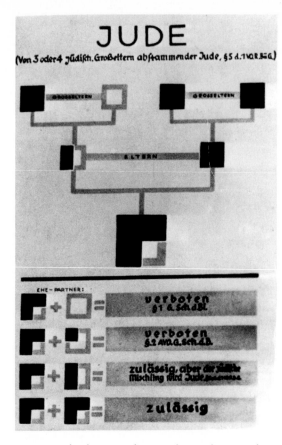

Diagram of "Who is Jewish" according to the Nuremberg Laws

protection. This law marked the beginning of the gradual loss of rights and the isolation of Jews in German society. The second law forbade marriage and sexual relations between Jews and Germans. Jews could not employ female Germans under the age of 45 nor display the German flag.

The Nuremberg Laws did not specifically define who was a Jew. This was left for the first "Regulation to the Reich Citizenship Law" of 14 November 1935. This law defined a "non-Aryan" as someone with either a Jewish parent or grandparent. Jews could be either full Jews, "half-Jews" or "quarter-Jews." Mainstream Nazi opinion called for treating half- and quarter-Jews as full Jews. There were some differences of opinion among Nazi leaders, however, as to how to treat half-Jews. Dr. Bernhard Loesener, a Nazi "racial expert" who helped write the law, said that the half-Jew was a "less serious enemy than the full Jew, because...he possesses so many German [characteristics]." In the end, a half-Jew was considered Jewish if he was married to a Jew or if he was part of the Jewish community.

The Nuremberg Laws gave legal form to the persecution of GERMANY's Jews, which had been started with the Nazi rise to power in 1933. They satisfied segments of the Nazi Party that were calling for strong ANTISEMITISM on the Party platform. The real horror was that the Nazis now had an effective legal weapon to carry out the isolation, destruction and plunder of the Jewish population. These laws became the legal tool of the "FINAL SOLUTION" and were applied in those countries taken over by the Germans.

NUREMBERG TRIALS

The major postwar trial of leading Nazis suspected of war crime, and of German organizations that were considered to be criminal. This was the first time that leaders of a country were tried by an international court for crimes that had been in keeping with state policy.

The trial opened in BERLIN on 18 October 1945 and adjourned to Nuremberg where judgment was handed down 30 September and 1 October 1946.

The defendants' box at the War Crimes Trial of Nazi leaders in Nuremberg. In the front row are (left to right) Hermann Göring, Rudolf Hess, Joachim von Ribbentrop, and Wilhelm Keitel; in the back row are (left to right Karl Donitz, Erich Raeder, Baldur von Schirach, Fritz Sauckel, and Alfred Jodl. They are surrounded by American military police

NUREMBERG TRIAL OF NAZI CRIMINALS

DEFENDANT	RANK	SENTENCE
Bormann, Martin (not present; whereabouts if alive—unknown)	Hitler's Deputy (from 1941)	Death
Dönitz, Karl	Admiral; Commander of Navy	Life imprisonment
Frank, Hans	Governor-General of Poland	Death
Frick, Wilhelm	Interior Minister	Death
Fritzsche, Hans	Broadcasting Head	Acquitted
Funk, Walther	President of Bank of Germany (until 1939)	Life imprisonment
Göring, Hermann	Reich Marshal; Commander-in-Chief of German Air Force	Death (but poisoned himself before sentence was carried out)
Hess, Rudolf	Hitler's Deputy (until 1941)	Life imprisonment
Jodl, Alfred	Army Chief of Operations	Death
Kaltenbrunner, Ernst	Chief of Security Police	Death
Keitel, Wilhelm	Field Marshal; Army Chief	Death
Neurath, Constantin von	Protector of Bohemia and Moravia	15 years imprisonment
Papen, Franz von	Ambassador to Austria, Turkey	Acquitted
Raeder, Erich	Navy Commander	Life imprisonment

(continued next page->)

NUREMBERG TRIAL OF NAZI CRIMINALS (continued)

DEFENDANT	RANK	SENTENCE
Ribbentrop, Joachim von	Foreign Minister	Death
Rosenberg, Alfred	Minister for the Occupied Eastern Territories	Death
Sauckel, Fritz	In charge of manpower	Death
Schacht, Hjalmar	Minister of Economics; President of Bank of Germany (until 1939)	Acquitted
Schirach, Baldur von	Nazi youth leader	20 years imprisonment
Seyss-Inquart, Arthur	Commissioner for Occupied Netherlands	Death
Speer, Albert	Minister for Armaments	20 years imprisonment
Streicher, Julius	Editor of Der Stürmer	Death

See also entries on individuals.

The International Military Tribunal (IMT) was established to conduct this trial. It consisted of eight judges, two each from the UNITED STATES, SOVIET RUSSIA, GREAT BRITAIN, and FRANCE. The Americans were strongly in favor of the trial, and it was conducted in their zone of occupation, in the German city of Nuremberg.

Twenty-two individuals were tried (see box). They were accused of three categories of crimes, namely: "Crimes Against Peace" (planning and waging wars of aggression, and conspiring to commit war crimes and crimes against humanity), "War Crimes" and "CRIMES AGAINST HUMANITY" (which included crimes against civilians and groups for which the laws of war offered no protection). Also charged were six organizations: the "Reich Cabinet," the "Leadership Corps of the Nazi Party," the

SS, the GESTAPO and SD ("Security Police"), the SA, and the "General Staff and High Command of the German Armed Forces."

The IMT sentenced 12 of the defendants to death, found 3 "not guilty" and sentenced the rest to various prison sentences. The Leadership Corps of the Nazi Party, the SS, the Gestapo and SD were declared to be "criminal organizations," meaning that individual members of these groups could later be tried as participants in crimes.

In its judgment, the IMT emphasized the fate of the Jews as the most clear-cut and extreme example of Nazi inhumanity. No other trial in history has covered so much detail. Its central theme was always the guilt in bringing about WORLD WAR II and the terrible crimes that this led to. For subsequent trials held at Nuremberg see TRIALS OF WAR CRIMALS.

OHLENDORF, OTTO

(1907–1951) Commander of EINSATZGRUPPEN-D, a division of the Nazi mobile killing units. These units operated in newly captured Soviet territory from 1941, killing more than 1.25 million JEWS and hundreds of thousands of Soviet prisoners of war and other Soviets.

Born in Hanover, Ohlendorf prepared for a distinguished career in economics and law. He studied at three universities, and held a doctorate in law. He was director of research of the Institute for World Economy and Maritime Transport in Kiel before he became commander of Einsatzgruppen-D. Even though he had joined the Nazi Party as early as 1925 and the ss in 1926, he was not a hoodlum. He was an academic and an intellectual.

After the war, he was the chief defendant in the Nuremberg Military Tribunals Case No. 9, in which

Otto Ohlendorf

PROSECUTOR: What were the instructions with respect to the Jews and the communist functionaries?

OHLENDORF: The instructions were that in the Russian operational areas of the Einsatzgruppen the Jews, as well as the Soviet political commissars, were to be liquidated.

PROSECUTOR: And when you say "liquidated," do you mean "killed"?

OHLENDORF: Yes, I mean " killed." In the late summer of 1941 [Heinrich] Himmler was in Nikolaiev. He assembled the leaders and men of the Einsatzkommandos, repeated to them the liquidation order, and pointed out that the leaders and men who were taking part in the liquidation bore no personal responsibility for the execution of this order. The responsibility was his, alone, and [Hitler's]....

To me it is inconceivable that a subordinate [secondary] leader should not carry out orders given by the leaders of the state.

PROSECUTOR: Was the legality of the orders explained to these people in a dishonest way?

OHLENDORF: I do not understand your question; since the order was issued by the superior authorities, the question of legality could not arise in the minds of these individuals, for they had sworn obedience to the people who had issued the orders.

From Otto Ohlendorf's testimony as the chief defendant in the Nuremberg Military Tribunals Case No. 9

the Einsatzgruppen were accused. His testimony is very revealing (see box). He was sentenced to death and hanged at Landsberg prison.

OLYMPIC GAMES OF 1936

Olympic Games held in GERMANY—in the winter in Garmisch-Partenkirchen and in the summer in BERLIN.

In 1931, the International Olympic Committee (IOC) decided to assign the 1936 games to Germany. When Adolf HITLER came to power in 1933, it was not at first clear if he would go ahead with the IOC's offer. It would mean hosting enemy powers, competing with JEWS and members of other "inferior" races, and appearing to support the international spirit of the Olympics. However, he also saw the Olympics as having great diplomatic opportunities for Germany. The excitement of showing off the new German order won out, and Hitler agreed to host the Games and to follow IOC rules.

In preparation for the event a new stadium was built. In addition, Berlin was cleaned up of antisemitic billboards and the pace of persecutions of Jews was slowed down. The half-Jewish fencer Helene Mayer and the Jewish ice-hockey player Rudi Ball were included in the German team, but only af-

American runner Jesse Owens starting the 200m race, which he won in a new Olympic record time of 20.7 seconds at the 1936 Berlin Olympic Games

> *Jesse Owens was originally scheduled to run in only three events. Two American Jewish runners, Marty Glickman and Sam Stoller, had qualified to run the 400-meter relay. The head of the United States National Olympic Committee, Avery Brundage, removed the two Jewish runners. He ordered Jesse Owens to run instead, since he was afraid of offending his German hosts. Owens's winning performance was viewed in America as a symbolic American victory over Nazi racism.*

ter pressure by the Americans. Another Jew, Captain Wolfgang Fürstner, was given the task of building and reorganizing the Olympic Village. Leni RIEFENSTAHL, the German film pioneer, filmed the games so that the Nazis could take full advantage of the PROPAGANDA value of the occasion.

The 1936 Olympics were the games in which the great African American sprinter, Jesse Owens, won four gold medals. However, Germany outscored the United States with 33 gold, 36 silver, and 30 bronze medals. On the diplomatic front, Hitler was able to use the games as a showcase for the new Germany. Hitler also succeeded in concealing from the world the awful truth of the Jewish persecution during the time of the games. In addition, Hitler's regular appearances at the stadium and the adoration of the crowds made a powerful impression on visitors. Captain Fürstner, who had been replaced at the last moment as chief of the Olympic Village because he was Jewish, attended the banquet honoring his successor after the Games, and then shot himself.

ONEG SHABBAT

SEE RINGELBLUM, EMANUEL AND ARCHIVES.

OPERATION BARBAROSSA

SEE BARBAROSSA, OPERATION.

ORGANIZATION TODT

The Nazi state construction organization named after Fritz Todt, an engineer and politician who had

Klooga camp in Estonia, run by Operation Todt, as it was found by Russian liberators

joined the NAZI PARTY in 1922. He had reached the higher levels of Nazi leadership by 1933. In December 1938 Todt was put in charge of the entire German building industry. His Todt Organization (or OT) was involved in building military facilities and railroads, and fortifying the Atlantic coast. It also rebuilt streets, bridges and railroad lines damaged in the fighting.

While the uniformed and regimented workers of the OT in GERMANY may have resembled the military, this was not the case in the occupied territories. There, particularly in locations close to CONCENTRATION CAMPS, tens of thousands of JEWS were employed as slave laborers. By 1940, in the areas surrounding WARSAW and LUBLIN alone, more than 30,000 Jews formed part of the OT work force. In keeping with the general Nazi aim of working the Jews to death, Jews were treated more harshly than the other foreign workers.

Todt died in a plane crash in 1942, and was succeeded by Albert SPEER.

O S T L A N D

("Eastern Territory")

PROPAGANDA term used by the Germans during WORLD WAR II. It refers to the Baltic countries (LITHUANIA, LATVIA, ESTONIA) and parts of BYELORUSSIA that were occupied by GERMANY after it invaded SOVIET RUSSIA in summer 1941.

The term had positive associations for Germans, since it reminded them of the German colonization of eastern Europe during the Middle Ages. At the same time, use of the term made it clear that in the future the area would remain under German rule. As in other occupied and annexed parts of eastern Europe, German leaders were mostly interested in using "Ostland" for the benefit of the German war effort. They also wanted to "Germanize" it. Mass killings of JEWS, GYPSIES, and communists started right after the German advance.

The EINSATZGRUPPEN (mobile killing units), as well as local police and the German military, combed the area. They especially targeted Jews in cities and towns. Many communities were destroyed in this first wave of killings. In Lithuania alone Einsatzgruppe A murdered more than 120,000 Jews by early 1942. More rural areas that had been left untouched in the first wave, were wiped out between spring 1942 and the German retreat in early 1944. The region of Ostland was liberated by the Soviet army by summer 1944.

p-q

P A L E S T I N E

Land in the Middle East, which was divided in 1948 into the State of ISRAEL and the Hashemite Kingdom of Jordan. After four centuries under Turkish rule, it was captured by the British in 1917. The British were then granted the Mandate (the right to rule it on trust) by the LEAGUE OF NATIONS. In 1917, the British issued the Balfour Declaration, which promised to establish a Jewish National Home in Palestine.

With the Nazi rise to power in 1933, thousands of German Jews fled to Palestine. This alarmed the Arabs in the country, who feared that one day the Jews would become a majority. To calm the Arabs, the British issued the WHITE PAPER OF 1939, which put severe limits on Jewish immigration. In response, the JEWS of Palestine (numbering 450,000 in 1939) organized ALIYA BET, which secretly brought refugees from Europe into the country. The British mounted a sea blockade to capture these Jews before they reached Palestine. Those caught were sent to detention camps in other lands (such as MAURITIUS, Kenya, and Eritrea in Africa, and CYPRUS).

During WORLD WAR II, the Jews of Palestine were forced to watch the systematic destruction of European Jewry without having the power to offer any real assistance to the victims. Their rescue efforts were very limited in scope, since they did not enjoy the support of either the British or American governments. They did fight the Germans, however, by joining the British army. In 1944, they were allowed to form the JEWISH BRIGADE GROUP.

After World War II, the Jews of Palestine became the leaders in the rescue of Jewish survivors from Europe. The struggle to open the gates of Palestine culminated in the establishment of the State of Israel on 14 May 1948. There, the survivors of the HOLOCAUST found a home at last.

Immigrants disembarking from SS Parita in Tel Aviv, 1939 under the watch of British soldiers

The seven Jewish parachutists who died:

Ben-Ya'akov, Zvi (1922–1944), captured in Slovakia, October 30, 1944, and executed by the Gestapo.

Berdicev, Abba (1918–1944), killed near Bratislava, Slovakia, while trying to lead a group of escaped Allied prisoners of war to safety.

Goldstein, Peretz (1923–1944), captured crossing the Hungarian border and executed.

Reik, Haviva (1914–1944), captured in Slovakia and executed by the Gestapo.

Reis, Raphael (1914–1944), captured in Slovakia and executed by the Gestapo.

Sereni, Haim Enzio (1905–1944), captured in Tuscany, Italy, and deported to Mauthausen, where he was executed.

Szenes, Hannah (1921–1944), captured in Hungary and executed after a trial for treason in Budapest.

PARACHUTISTS, JEWISH

Military means advocated and used by the leadership of the Jewish underground army in PALESTINE (the *Hagana*) to rescue European Jewry, after news of the "FINAL SOLUTION" became known to the Jewish community in Palestine. Since the *Hagana* lacked the resources to carry out the mission alone, they

Jewish parachutists from Palestine before being dropped by the British army behind enemy lines in Europe

persuaded the British secret service to become in-volved. The British approached the JEWISH AGENCY with a proposal to train a group of Palestinian volunteers who would be dropped by parachute behind enemy lines in the Balkans for espionage and other activities. The Jewish Agency leaders believed that the paratroopers would also be able to fulfil their Jewish and Zionist mission to rescue Jewish survivors.

Of 250 volunteers, 32 were chosen. The majority were former refugees and recent immigrants, members of the *Palmach*, the *Hagana*'s striking arm. Although they operated in several countries and some fought hard in the SLOVAK NATIONAL UPRISING, the mission of the paratroopers did not live up to either its military or rescue potential. However, it did serve as an important rallying point for European JEWS.

The brave action of these men and women showed that the Jews of Palestine cared enough to risk life and limb to attempt rescue missions when the rest of the world showed little interest or concern. Since the end of WORLD WAR II, the mission of the paratroopers has attained near legendary status in Israel and among Jewish communities throughout the world.

Twelve of the parachutists fell into Nazi hands; seven of them died in captivity or were executed as spies.

P A R I S

Capital of FRANCE. Paris was occupied by German forces in June 1940 and liberated in August 1944. In 1939, 200,000 JEWS were living there.

After the June 1940 cease-fire with GERMANY, Paris became the capital of German-occupied France. From the beginning of the occupation, Jewish property was confiscated and Jews were subject to an increasing number of humiliating restrictions. Some Jews had escaped, but 150,000 remained in the city. In June 1942, it was decreed that all Jews living in the occupied zone aged six and over had to wear the Jewish BADGE: a yellow star of David marked *Juif* or *Juive* ("Jew"). Public response in Paris to the yellow star was actively hostile. For this reason, the Germans decided not to impose the wearing of the yellow star in the southern zone of France, even after they occupied the whole of France in 1942.

On 1 July 1942, Adolf EICHMANN visited Paris to set the final plans for the first massive round-up and DEPORTATION of Jews. On 16 July 1942, some 13,000 Jewish men, women, and children were rounded up by French police from five sections of Paris and taken to the sports stadium known as the *Vélodrome d'Hiver*, or *Vel d'Hiv*, in central Paris. Around 100 committed suicide. The rest were sent the following morning to the internment camp at

The arrest and round-up of Jews in Paris, August 1941

DRANCY, in a northeastern suburb of Paris. From there, most were deported to their deaths at AUSCHWITZ. Approximately 50,000 Paris Jews died in the HOLOCAUST.

P A R T I S A N S

Groups of organized guerilla fighters who aimed to damage the German war effort by attacking military targets.

The partisans often used forests for cover. They received some support from local people in towns and on farms. This assisted the partisans in their attack against the Germans and their helpers.

Partisans who fought the Germans in eastern Europe generally included both the ultra-nationalists and the socialist-leftists. The ultra-nationalist groups wanted to be rid of all foreigners who invaded their soil. This included both the Germans and the JEWS. The socialist-leftists were dedicated to fighting FASCISM. They were supported by SOVIET RUSSIA and were dedicated to defeating the Nazis and driving them from their homeland. For non-Jews the reasons for becoming a partisan were national or personal. For Jews the reasons were revenge or to save themselves.

There were many Jewish partisan fighters. Some of them escaped from the GHETTOS. They made their way to the forests to try to join the partisans in fighting the Nazis. The ultra-nationalist partisans

Never say that you have come to your journey's end,
When the days turn black, and clouds upon our world descend,
Believe the dark will lift, and freedom yet appear.
Our marching feet will tell the world that we are here.

beginning of the *"Song of the Partisans"* (written in Yiddish), a favorite song of the Jewish anti-Nazi partisans

were often almost as antisemitic as the Nazis, often even murdering Jews who crossed their path. Jews who came across socialist-leftist partisan groups fared much better since they were more open to strangers—including Jews.

Jewish partisans were willing to join groups that would accept them. Some groups of Jews collectively joined partisan forces as a unit. Jewish partisans fought in YUGOSLAVIA, BULGARIA, GREECE, POLAND, LITHUANIA, SLOVAKIA, FRANCE, ITALY, BYELORUSSIA, the UKRAINE, and Soviet Russia.

Jews took tremendous risks when they tried to link up with partisan units. When individual Jews or

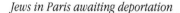
Jews in Paris awaiting deportation

Entrance to hideout of Jewish partisans in Rudninkai forest, Lithuania

Jewish groups hid in the forests, they were often informed on or turned over to the Nazis by local farmers and peasants. When they found friendly partisan units or contacts, they were sometimes rejected as members. This is because those wishing to join a partisan unit had to have both military experience and a weapon. Even when Jewish fighters presented themselves with arms, the weapons were sometimes

Yugoslav partisans

seized along with their clothing and food. Rejection from a unit meant certain death, since partisan groups had to guard their secrecy.

Despite these obstacles, there were a handful of Jewish partisan units. The most famous were the Bielski Partisans, run by four Jewish BIELSKI brothers: Tuvia, Zusya, Asael, and Aharon. Their unit was located between VILNA and MINSK in the Naliboki forest in Byelorussia. Another famous group was named Uncle Misha, after Misha Gildenman. It was located in the Ukraine. In the Rudninkai forest, just outside Vilna, Lithuania, Abba KOVNER's Struggle for Victory and Revenge Unit was another active group. It is estimated that approximately 15,000 Jews were partisan fighters in Soviet-sponsored units.

"P A T R I A"

Boat carrying Jewish refugees from Europe, which sank in PALESTINE's Haifa Bay in 1940 with a large loss of life.

The British had limited Jewish immigration to Palestine and set up a blockade. Palestinian Jews were desperate to rescue Jews from the HOLOCAUST. They organized the "illegal" ALIYA BET to bring Jews

"Illegal" immigrants on board the S.S. Patria before its sinking

into the country, despite the orders of the British. In early November 1940, the British captured three "illegal" boats carrying Jewish refugees. The British policy was to deport the passengers to the island of MAURITIUS in the Indian Ocean. Since two of the boats were considered unseaworthy, the immigrants from those ships were transferred to the *Patria*, a ship that the British had captured earlier. The Jewish Palestine underground, the Hagana, tried to prevent the deportation. It smuggled explosives onto the *Patria*, hoping to disable the boat's engine. However, the ship was not in good physical condition. The resulting explosion sank the ship in less than 15 minutes. Of the 1,771 persons aboard, 267 were killed and another 172 were injured.

Despite this tragedy, plans were still made for deporting the *Patria* survivors. This attempt was canceled because of the outcry from influential leaders in Palestine and England, including Prime Minister Winston CHURCHILL. He convinced the Palestine government to let the immigrants stay in prison in Palestine. Although they were imprisoned at first, most *Patria* survivors were released in 1941.

PAVELIC, ANTE

(1889–1959) Leader of the fascist puppet state of CROATIA. He was elected to the Yugoslav parliament for the Croatian Justice Party in 1929. However, when King Alexander of YUGOSLAVIA established a dictatorship in the country, Ante Pavelic fled to ITALY. There he founded the USTASHA, an underground organization that waged a terrorist campaign to win Croatia's independence. He modeled the movement's program on Italian fascism and Nazi antisemitism.

With the conquest of Yugoslavia by GERMANY in 1941, Croatia was granted nominal independence under Pavelic and the Ustasha. One of his first measures was to confiscate Jewish property in Zagreb. Pavelic's new government sought to "purge Croatia of foreign elements," especially Serbs and JEWS. It established a brutal regime with a network of DEATH CAMPS, where victims were shot or starved to death. Other "enemies of the state," including many Croatians opposed to the regime, were thrown off cliffs, beaten to death, or burned alive in their homes. In June 1941, Pavelic issued a special decree declaring that the Jews, "well-known black marketeers that

Ante Pavelic

they are," were collectively responsible for stirring up the population. Hundreds of thousands were killed in Croatia and Bosnia-Herzegovina. After the war, Pavelic fled to Argentina, where he continued to call for Croatian independence. He died in 1959 as a result of injuries suffered in an attempt on his life two years earlier.

PEHLE, JOHN W.

(1909–) United States official. Born in Minneapolis, Minnesota, Pehle went to Washington in 1934 and joined the staff of the Treasury Department. He worked with the Foreign Exchange Control Division before becoming an assistant to Secretary of the Treasury Henry J. MORGENTHAU, Jr., in 1940.

Pehle was placed in charge of the Foreign Funds Control, an office that became more important after WORLD WAR II began. Its purpose during the war was to prevent the enemy from being able to seize foreign funds in countries it had captured and to protect the investments of occupied countries in the United States.

At meetings he attended, he learned about State Department policy, which blocked the rescue of JEWS in Europe. This prompted him to draft an important memo in December 1943, together with Morgenthau's assistant, Josiah DuBois, Jr., and Randolph Paul, the general counsel of the Department of the Treasury. The memo was entitled "Report to the Secretary on the Acquiescence (Passive Acceptance) of This Government in the Murder of the Jews." The memo charged State Department officials with preventing the rescue of Jews and with blocking the flow of information concerning the murder of the Jewish population in Europe. It also charged that these officials tried to cover up their guilt by "concealment and misrepresentation," "the giving of false and misleading explanations for their failures to act" and issuing "false and misleading statements."

After the memo was shortened and toned down, it was presented to President Franklin D. ROOSEVELT by Secretary Morgenthau in January 1944. Roosevelt agreed to establish the WAR REFUGEE BOARD (WRB) to improve American efforts at rescue. Pehle was assigned to direct its activities. Morgenthau described Pehle as "young, dynamic, bold, clear, and a bit brash."

Under Pehle's leadership, the WRB tried to find a haven for Jews, evacuate Jews from German-occupied territories, send supplies to CONCENTRATION CAMPS, and threaten German leaders and their allies with TRIALS OF WAR CRIMINALS if they participated in the murder of Jews. Pehle also unsuccessfully pressed for the AUSCHWITZ BOMBING.

Through its agents in SWITZERLAND, SWEDEN, North Africa, ITALY, Turkey and, most importantly, BUDAPEST, the WRB played a crucial role in saving as many as 200,000 Jews. Yet when Pehle viewed the work of the WRB after 12 years of American efforts, he commented: "What we did was little enough. It was late. Late and little, I would say."

PÉTAIN, MARSHAL HENRI PHILIPPE

(1856–1951) French World War I military hero who led the VICHY government, which collaborated with the Germans in WORLD WAR II.

Pétain became a military hero defending the fortress of Verdun in World War I. He was made a

Marshal Henri Philippe Pétain

marshal of FRANCE in 1918 and became the symbol of victory for the French people. After France fell to the Germans in 1940, Pétain was called to head the new French government at Vichy, which ruled over the southern part of France, not occupied by the Germans. Pétain's charisma, military reputation, and popularity with the French population led to widespread acceptance of his leadership. This was based on faith in his strong patriotism and his urge to save the honor of the defeated France. When he was voted prime minister with full powers, he was already 84 years old.

The Vichy government, headed by Pétain and assisted by Pierre LAVAL, cooperated fully with the Germans. This included supporting their anti-Jewish policies, particularly in the DEPORTATION of the Jewish population from France. Pétain was largely a figurehead after April 1942, when Laval became head of government.

After the liberation of France in 1944, Pétain was found guilty of treason and sentenced to death. The sentence was later commuted to life imprisonment due to his record of valor during World War I. Pétain spent the last years of his life imprisoned on the Ile d'Yeu, an island off the coast of Brittany in northern France.

PIONEER FIGHTERS

("*He-Halutz ha-Lohem*")

Name of the armed RESISTANCE organization in KRAKÓW, composed mainly of Zionist youth.

The Kraków fighters had a close relationship with their comrades-in-arms in WARSAW, the JEWISH FIGHTING ORGANIZATION. The Pioneer Fighters chose to remain a very small and secretive group so that they could maintain high security and efficiency.

They did not attack German targets within the GHETTO. Instead, they chose to escape and to strike at the Nazis outside the ghetto and then return to the "safety" within. They did this in order to protect the other ghetto residents from the German practice of collective punishment. If it had been discovered that an armed resistance movement existed in the ghetto, the Nazis would have murdered hundreds or thousands in order to force the fighters to give themselves up.

The Pioneer Fighters sabotaged train lines, blew up German warehouses, and stole weapons from German soldiers. The high point of their activities took place on 22 December 1942, in the center of the German-controlled old city of Kraków. The Pioneer Fighters tossed a bomb into the Ciganeria Cafe, a popular hangout for Nazi officers, and then returned to the ghetto. The explosion was one of the most successful raids against the Nazis. It resulted in the death and injury of many German officers. The non-Jewish partisans were blamed and took credit for the attack. Until recently, the plaque placed on the site after the war did not mention the Jewish fighters.

After the Ciganeria Cafe raid, the Germans discovered a large group of the Pioneer Fighters and killed them. The remaining Pioneer Fighters then ceased activities in the city of Kraków and continued their resistance in nearby forests for a few more months.

PIUS XII

(1876–1959) Pope from 1939 until his death. His failure to issue any public condemnation of the

Holocaust during WORLD WAR II has stirred up widespread controversy. Born Eugenio Pacelli, he was the Papal Nuncio (ambassador) in GERMANY during the 1920s. In 1933, when he was secretary of state of the Vatican, he signed an agreement with Nazi Germany, which was a diplomatic triumph for Adolf HITLER.

Pius's "silence" during World War II has been linked to his deep fear of communist expansion, which led him to regard Hitler as a protector against Soviet inroads into Europe. Some say that he felt that any public condemnation of Hitler and his policies would lead to reprisals against Catholic clergy and believers in countries under Nazi domination. His accusers point out that the Church had a religious and moral duty to speak out and should not have been swayed by other considerations in such a clear-cut issue of right and wrong. They criticize him not only for his silence on the HOLOCAUST but on many aspects of Hitler's policies, such as his persecution of the Catholic clergy in POLAND. They feel that a public statement by the Pope would have carried great weight and could have had an effect on Nazi policies.

Pius's defenders, on the other hand, point to the dilemma in which he was placed. They also refer to actions by Catholic clergy in a number of European countries to help or save the JEWS, including the Pope's own behind-the-scenes efforts in ITALY, where a large section of the Jewish community was protected and saved by the Catholic Church (see also CHURCHES).

P L A S Z Ó W

FORCED LABOR camp on the outskirts of KRAKÓW. It was built at the end of 1942, part of it over two old Jewish cemeteries. After the liquidation of the Kraków GHETTO in March 1943, most of the city's remaining 6,000–8,000 JEWS were transferred there. At its peak, Plaszów housed over 20,000 prisoners, including Jews, Poles, and GYPSIES. Camp inmates worked at producing glass, metal, clothing and brushes for the Germans.

Amon GOETH, the sadistic commandant of the camp, murdered Jews at his whim. Following his lead, other guards were particularly cruel in their behavior toward the Jews. It is difficult to know how many people died at Plaszów, but estimates place the number at about 8,000. Many more were

Jews gathering garbage in Plaszów concentration camp

transferred to DEATH CAMPS to be killed. Those who died at Plaszów were buried in huge pits. Later, as the end of the war was in sight, the pits were opened and the bodies burned to remove evidence of the mass murders (see AKTION 1005). Approximately 2,000 Jews survived Plaszów, nearly half of those through the efforts of Oskar SCHINDLER. Schindler employed them at his nearby enamelware factory, which he moved to Sudetenland in CZECHOSLOVAKIA together with his Jewish workers.

Today, only small green hills remain at the site of the camp. Two monuments also stand there—a small one erected soon after the war by Jewish survivors from Kraków and a large one established by the Polish communists in the 1960s.

The Jewish memorial at Plaszów reads:

"Here, in this area, have been tortured, murdered and turned into ashes thousands of Jews during the years 1943–1945, who were driven here from all over Poland and Hungary. We do not know the names of the murdered. Let us replace them with only one word— Jews.... Language has no words to define the atrocity of this crime, its nightmarish bestiality, ruthlessness and cruelty. Let us replace it with one word—Nazism. In commemoration of those murdered here, whose last cry of despair is the silence of this Plaszów cemetery, we, Jews saved from the fascist pogrom, pay homage."

PLOT TO KILL HITLER

Conspiracy by a number of top German military men to take the life of Adolf HITLER at his headquarters on 20 July 1944.

There had been several earlier attempts on Hitler's life during the year leading up to the one of 20 July 1944. All of them had failed. At one point, a bomb had been placed among brandy bottles on Hitler's airplane but it had failed to go off. On other occasions, an overcoat had been outfitted with

bombs, again without success. There were two key factors that seemed to encourage this treason. First, it became increasingly clear that Germany could not win the war. Second, many within the military and the inner circles of Nazi power had begun to doubt Hitler's stability. The Allied invasion of Europe, on 6 June 1944, strengthened the resolve of the conspirators to take action against Hitler.

The key conspirator in the 20 July assassination attempt was Count Claus von Stauffenberg, a respected lieutenant colonel who had been seriously wounded in Tunisia when his vehicle ran over a mine. He lost an eye, his right hand, and two fingers from his left hand. Upon recovering from his wounds, he was reassigned to the General Army Office in Berlin. Von Stauffenberg was able to put together a group of conspirators who would form a new anti-Nazi government if the assassination attempt met with success. They would also seize control of the military. By the time he had finished, the cast of conspirators included prominent generals and politicians, such as Carl Goerdeler, Mayor of Leipzig, and Field Marshal Erwin Rommel, the outstanding general, now commander, of Army group B in western Europe. However Rommel was opposed to killing Hitler.

The new plan (popularly known as the "Generals' Plot"), was ready by the end of 1943. It included naming Goerdeler as chancellor after the coup. Allied successes both in the west and the east forced the conspirators to take action. When von Stauffenberg was promoted to the position of chief of staff of the Home Army, it gave him easy access to Hitler. It became clear to all the conspirators, that von Stauffenberg would be the assassin and that the time was at hand. On 15 July, there was another near miss. Finally, five days later, von Stauffenberg carried a bomb with him into a personal meeting with Hitler at his headquarters in Rangsdorf, East Prussia. He slid his briefcase containing the explosive to within six feet of Hitler. After von Stauffenberg slipped away from the meeting, the briefcase was accidentally moved out of range for killing Hitler. Though many of the men present at the meeting were killed in the explosion, Hitler was virtually uninjured. He kept repeating, "Think of it. Nothing has happened to me. This is further proof that Fate has chosen me for my mission."

Klaus von Stauffenberg

It became known very quickly that von Stauffenberg had left the meeting early, and was the source of the explosion. His arrest and that of his co-conspirators took place within the day. By 1 a.m. the following morning, he was executed along with several others, some of them hanged on meat hooks. In consideration of his popularity, Rommel was allowed to commit suicide. There was a bloodbath in the weeks that followed. The purge following the attempt on Hitler's life was brutal in the extreme. Loyal Nazis acted without mercy against fellow German citizens.

The unsuccessful coup of June 1944 was the most serious challenge to Hitler's power during the 12-year history of the THIRD REICH.

P O G R O M

A Russian word meaning "attack." It was first used to mean assaults on Jewish communities by mobs, which were organized by the Russian government in the late nineteenth and early twentieth centuries. After the Russian Civil War (1917–1921), pogroms no longer occurred in Russia. They were reintroduced by the Nazis. The name was given to the

KRISTALLNACHT outrages all over GERMANY and AUSTRIA in November 1938, in which Jews were attacked and killed. During these pogroms, many Jews were also sent to CONCENTRATION CAMPS, and synagogues and Jewish property were looted and burned to the ground. Following Kristallnacht, the word was used for local assaults in which Jews and their property were brutally attacked by Germans and other antisemites.

P O H L ,   O S W A L D

(1892–1951) SS lieutenant-general who was responsible for the profit-making aspects of the murder of the JEWS.

Pohl developed the economic strength of the SS while working as ministerial director of the Ministry of the Interior during 1939–1942. He then headed the SS Economic and Administrative Head Office. Among other functions, this office became responsible for the running of the CONCENTRATION CAMPS, specifically for using the FORCED LABOR of the inmates. These slave-laborers worked in SS factories and businesses and numbered up to half a million people. Pohl's office allocated laborers to the industries it favored. It also channeled the property of murdered Jews, including their gold fillings, into SS treasuries. In 1943, Pohl was also placed at the head of SS enterprise using Jewish labor in the General-gouvernement, which established five plants employing over 14,000 additional forced laborers. After the war, in 1946, Pohl was discovered in hiding. He was tried in 1947 and executed for his war crimes.

P O L A N D

Country in eastern Europe. In 1939, more than three million JEWS were living in Poland. For centuries it had been the greatest center of Jewish life in the world with a rich communal, religious, and cultural life. All this ended when the Germans invaded Poland on 1 September 1939, beginning WORLD WAR II. The Germans soon conquered the country. Poland was divided on 28 September between GERMANY and the Soviets, according to an agreement reached with SOVIET RUSSIA a few days before the outbreak of war (the NAZI-SOVIET PACT). The Russians took over eastern Poland and the Germans took the rest of the country. The Soviets did not ac-

Oswald Pohl (first right on the lower row) together with the heads of the SS administration on trial in Nuremberg

tively persecute the Jews. In the two months before the borders between the two sections could be firmly set, a quarter of a million Jews from German-

occupied Poland escaped to the Soviet side.

The Germans annexed the parts of Poland closest to Germany, which became part of the THIRD REICH.

Jewish police searching an elderly Jew in Poland

In the Warsaw Ghetto

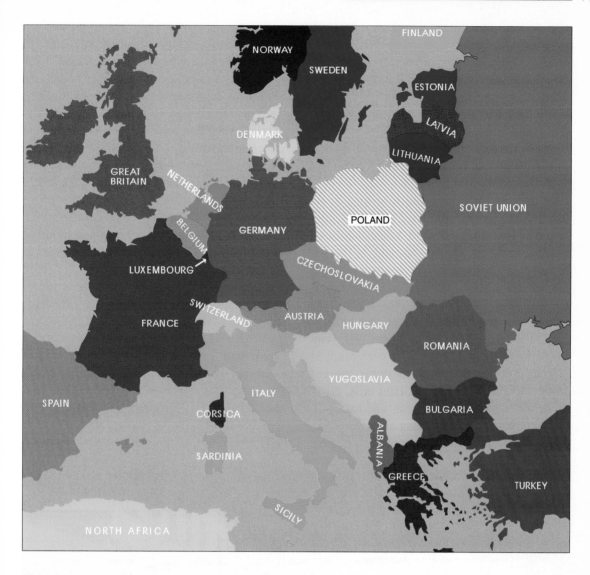

The entire center of former Poland was made into a special province called the GENERALGOUVERNEMENT (General Government) under a Nazi governor. Its capital was in KRAKÓW. A million and a half Jews were concentrated in its territory. The Nazis chose this area of Poland for their most systematic program to murder European Jewry.

During the fighting of September 1939, 20,000 Jews were killed and tens of thousands of Jewish businesses destroyed in Poland. The Germans lost no time in carrying out their anti-Jewish policies. On 8 October, the first GHETTO was established at Piotrków. By the end of the year, many measures had been taken against the Jews, including massacres. Ghettos were set up, including the one in WARSAW, which became the largest ghetto with al-most half a million inhabitants. These were populated not only by the Jews from the town itself, but from the entire vicinity. The rural areas and villages were soon empty of Jews. Jewish Councils (see JU-DENRAT) were appointed to be responsible for the Jew-ish communities. They were strictly supervised by the Nazis. Jews were deported in large numbers to the Generalgouvernement from other parts of Poland. They were subject to an ever growing list of humili-ating laws. They were robbed of their belongings and sent to do FORCED LABOR in LABOR CAMPS. By 1940, walls were built around the ghettos to prevent any contact between Jews and the "Aryan" population. The Warsaw ghetto was totally sealed off by Novem-ber 1940.

At first, the Nazis developed a plan for expelling

large number of Jews to the area of LUBLIN (see NISKO AND LUBLIN PLAN). Tens of thousands of Jews from the expanded Reich and the WARTHEGAU area were sent there. They lived in terrible conditions in transit camps. After a time, the project was dropped, but not before many Jews died. They were either killed or died from sickness and starvation. German soldiers frequently subjected the Jews to mass shootings, and almost 100,000 had been murdered by the end of 1940.

On 22 June 1941, the Germans invaded Soviet Russia. The very next day, they began the mass murder of Jews, using the mobile killing units called EINSATZGRUPPEN. This was the beginning of the systematic Nazi campaign for the destruction of the Jews of Europe. As the Germans occupied town after town, the Einsatzgruppen shot hundreds of thousands of Jews. In many places, they were assisted by local COLLABORATORS. By August 1941, Reinhard HEYDRICH wrote that "it may be safely assumed that there will be no more Jews in the annexed Eastern territories." In October, Hans FRANK, governor of the Generalgouvernement, told his ministers that all the Jews were being done away with. To speed the process, the major DEATH CAMPS were set up in this area and the method of killing be-

came primarily gassing in vans and GAS CHAMBERS.

The Jews in the ghettos of Poland lived in terrible conditions of overcrowding and starvation. Many died from hunger and disease. Yet within the ghetto they fought to preserve sparks of humanity. They tried to maintain a communal, religious, educational, and cultural life. The younger people were organized in YOUTH MOVEMENTS and formed UNDERGROUND cells to plan desperate and hopeless RESISTANCE efforts. Some tried to escape. A number of these were assisted or hidden by non-Jews (see "RIGHTEOUS AMONG THE NATIONS"). Others found their efforts blocked by antisemitic Poles. Some Jews fought in the Polish and Soviet armies. Others escaped to the forests and joined the PARTISANS.

DEPORTATIONS of groups of ghetto residents to death camps began in late 1941. The first death camp opened at CHELMNO on 8 December 1941. On 26 March 1942, the first Jews arrived in AUSCHWITZ. AKTION REINHARD involved the founding of three major death camps—TREBLINKA, SOBIBÓR and BELZEC—within the Generalgouvernement. The two million Jews then living in the Generalgouvernement were sent to their deaths. News of the fate of the deported Jews filtered back to the ghettos, and armed resistance began. The most famous of these revolts was

View of the main street in the Lódz Ghetto

the WARSAW GHETTO UPRISING in spring 1943. Jewish fighters in the ghetto held out against the Germans for several weeks. There were armed revolts in twenty ghettos and in five death camps.

The merciless killing process continued. By early 1944, no ghettos remained. Heinrich HIMMLER boasted that this was a page of glory in German history. Fewer than 400,000 Polish Jews remained alive when Poland was liberated by the Soviet army in 1944–1945. Many of these had found refuge in Soviet Russia from where they returned after the war.

Most of the survivors decided that there was no future for them in bloodsoaked Poland. This feeling became stronger as they faced continued ANTI-SEMITISM, and especially after the KIELCE pogrom of July 1946, in which 42 Jews were murdered. Most of the remaining Jews of Poland chose to leave. They found new homes in ISRAEL, the United States, and other countries. By 1947, only 80,000 Jews were living in Poland. Later, anti-Jewish campaigns drove many of these away. By the 1980s, fewer than 10,000 Jews were left in this former great Jewish center.

P O N A R Y

Mass killing site located some six miles from VILNA in

> *All the Gestapo roads lead to Ponary and Ponary means death.*
>
> Abba Kovner in his call to the Vilna Resistance on 31 December 1941

LITHUANIA. There, German EINSATZGRUPPEN (mobile killing units) and their Lithuanian collaborators murdered the JEWS of Vilna and neighboring towns and villages.

During their occupation of Lithuania in 1940–1941, Soviet Russian forces had dug large pits for fuel storage tanks. They were forced to flee when the Germans invaded SOVIET RUSSIA in June 1941, and the project was left incomplete.

The Germans had another use for this site. It became the burial place for tens of thousands of Jews as well as Soviet prisoners of war and political commissars murdered by the Einsatzgruppen. Beginning in July 1941, Jews from Vilna and the vicinity were rounded up and brought to Ponary by foot or by rail. Upon arrival, they were taken to pits and shot.

In September 1943, the Germans returned to Ponary and other massacre sites. They assigned a

Jews herded for execution by a Lithuanian militia in Ponary, 1941

SONDERKOMMANDO unit of 80 prisoners to dig up the bodies and burn them. They wanted to destroy all evidence of their crimes before they were discovered by the advancing Soviet army. These prisoners knew that they too would be killed on the completion of their terrible task. They made a daring escape attempt on 15 April 1944. Most of them were killed. Fifteen escaped to the nearby forest, where they joined PARTISAN units.

No one knows the exact number of Jews killed at Ponary, but it has been estimated at between 70,000 and 100,000.

Today, the site is marked by a monument. The pits are filled up and marked by flower beds. The ramp built by the Germans where they sorted the bodies still stands. The railroad tracks still pass the site.

P O N I A T O W A

Polish prison and LABOR CAMP and the scene of one of the largest massacres of Jewish prisoners during WORLD WAR II. The camp was set up in the fall of 1941 in the town of Poniatowa, not far from LUBLIN. At first it was for SOVIET PRISONERS OF WAR. Due to Reinhard HEYDRICH's policy of "extermination through work," more than 20,000 Russian prisoners of war died there in less than a year. Jewish prisoners began to arrive in October 1942.

The survivors of the WARSAW ghetto were sent to Poniatowa in March 1943. Although precise numbers are unknown, an estimated 15,000 to 20,000 Jews were resettled there. Conditions were very harsh.

The Ukrainian guards at Poniatowa tortured and executed prisoners. A new UNDERGROUND movement was set up by the JEWISH FIGHTING ORGANIZATION. Its aim was to stage an uprising before the camp was destroyed. However, the underground fighters lacked arms and ammunition. In November 1943, the Nazis decided to destroy the camp. The operation, cynically code-named "Harvest Festival" (see ERNTEFEST) took place during the night of 3–4 November.

The prisoners were led out of the barracks and machine gunned. More than 15,000 were killed that night. Those who refused to leave the barracks were burned alive. Only a handful managed to escape.

P O R T U G A L

Country bordering the Atlantic Ocean in western Europe. Like neighboring SPAIN, Portugal had a long history of ANTISEMITISM. Fewer than 400 Jews were living in Portugal on the eve of WORLD WAR II. This number increased when some 700 Jewish refugees from other parts of Europe were allowed in as "residents" before the onset of the war.

Portugal remained neutral during the war. However, it let Jewish refugees cross its territory to safety. These included trainloads of French Jews fleeing VICHY FRANCE. Portugal soon became one of the gateways to America and to PALESTINE. An estimated 30,000 Jews sailed to safety from the ports of Spain and Portugal. A number of international Jewish organizations were allowed to set up offices in Lisbon, the capital of Portugal. The AMERICAN JEWISH JOINT DISTRIBUTION COMMITTEE had its main office and center of operations for Europe in Lisbon. The WAR REFUGEE BOARD also had offices there. Thus, many operations to save and aid JEWS were channeled through Portugal during the HOLOCAUST. Portugal was one of the countries that granted passports to Hungarian Jews and the 698 passports it gave them saved that many lives.

P R A C O V N Á   S K U P I N A

see WORKING GROUP.

P R A G U E

Capital of CZECHOSLOVAKIA. In the early 1930s, 35,000 Jews were living in Prague. After Adolf HITLER's rise to power in 1933, many German Jews fled to Prague. In 1938, Jews from AUSTRIA and the Sudetenland fled to the city. This increased the Jewish population to about 55,000.

GERMANY occupied Prague on 15 March 1939. In July, Adolf EICHMANN arrived to open the Nazis' Central Office for Jewish Emigration. Eichmann's goal was to rid Prague of its JEWS. A considerable number managed to escape to other countries before the outbreak of war.

When the war broke out in September 1939, Jewish leaders were rounded up and arrested. In February 1943 the German authorities ordered the Jew-

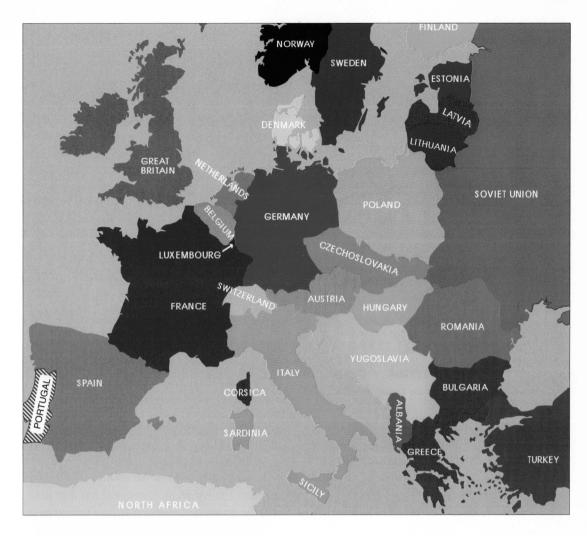

ish leaders to set up a JUDENRAT (Jewish Council).

Between October 1941 and March 1945, the Nazis deported all of Prague's 46,000 Jews. Most of them were sent first to nearby THERESIENSTADT, and then to their deaths in AUSCHWITZ. After the Jews were deported, their land and property were taken or sold. Synagogues and other large buildings were turned into warehouses.

Prague became the storage center of a large collection of Jewish ritual objects that the Nazis had plundered from Jewish families and institutions all over Europe. The Nazis planned to establish a "Museum of the Vanished Jewish Race" after their victory. Tens of thousands of items—Torah Scrolls and other ritual objects—were collected and stored.

Physically, the Jewish Quarter—with its famous ancient synagogues, buildings and cemetery—was not touched during the war. The old Jewish Quarter is now maintained by a tiny community, but it attracts many tourists—non-Jews as well as Jews—who have a rare chance to view the grandeur that once belonged to the community. The thousands of ritual objects that the Nazis had stolen form an exhibit called "The Precious Legacy," now displayed in the ancient synagogues. On the walls of the Pinkas synagogue are inscribed the names of the 77,000 Jews of BOHEMIA AND MORAVIA killed by the Nazis.

PRESIDENT'S ADVISORY COMMITTEE ON POLITICAL REFUGEES (PACPR)

Body created by President Franklin D. ROOSEVELT in April 1938, to advise the United States government about REFUGEE policies and to coordinate the work of private refugee organizations in the United

The German army entering Prague Castle, 15 March 1939

States. The committee's members were appointed by Roosevelt, with James G. McDonald (formerly the LEAGUE OF NATIONS high commissioner for refugees) serving as chairman. Most of its small budget came from the AMERICAN JEWISH JOINT DISTRIBUTION COMMITTEE, yet it was still considered a Presidential Committee.

After the EVIAN CONFERENCE, the PACPR explored several plans that had been suggested for solving the refugee crisis. Each plan looked for ways to create a large haven for refugees in remote areas of the world. Investigators were sent to three areas with the support of the United States and British governments: Mindanao (Philippine Islands), British Guiana (Guyana), and the Dominican Republic.

The committee also played an important role in a special immigration program, which was created by the Roosevelt administration after the fall of FRANCE in 1940. It allowed some 2,000 political and intellectual refugees to enter the United States by getting around existing laws.

The PACPR continually tried to persuade Roosevelt and the American Congress to ease immigration laws and admission procedures. It had several clashes with the State Department over immigration policies. In September 1940, the special immigration program was almost closed. This was because the State Department argued that it allowed potential traitors to enter the country disguised as refugees. The PACPR protested, and was able to extend the program until mid-1941 on a limited basis. In July 1941, the State Department cut immigration quotas. After failing to convince Roosevelt, the PACPR persuaded the State Department to establish an appeals system for rejected visa applications.

The committee's activities declined sharply after the United States entered the war on 8 December 1941. Of its 61 meetings, only 10 were held after this date. In September 1942, the PACPR played a key role in an attempt to save 5,000 Jewish CHILDREN in France, whose parents had been deported to POLAND. Although the United States government issued visas for the children, the Nazis did not permit them to leave.

PROPAGANDA, NAZI

Manipulation of public opinion and attitudes. The Nazis used propaganda more effectively than any other organization in history.

„Die Judennaſe iſt an ihrer Spitze gebogen. Sie ſieht aus wie ein Sechſer..."

Page from the antisemitic German children's book, "The Poisonous Mushroom." The text reads, "The Jewish nose is crooked at its tip. It looks like the number six..."

At first, propaganda was a means for the Nazis to gain support within GERMANY. Once in power, though, the goal of Nazi propaganda changed. It turned to strengthening Adolf HITLER's dictatorship

over the population. This meant stimulating nationalistic and racist feelings among German citizens. This goal was expanded to include support
for Germany's complete dominance over the
world.

The major economic and social downfall of Germany after World War I had led Germans to look
for radical solutions to their problems. The strong
emotional appeal of Nazi propaganda, and Hitler's
political appeal, seemed to provide all the answers.

Propaganda does not make use of clear political
or intellectual arguments. The Nazis' technique was
to use misinformation, racial stereotypes, and bla-
tant lies to appeal to the emotions of the masses.
According to Minister of Propaganda Josef GOEBBELS,
its aim was to "win the hearts of the people and
keep them."

This often meant using violence and intimidation
by groups like the SA, SS, and GESTAPO. Goebbels's
propaganda machine also aimed at establishing a
major enemy for the German people to focus on—
the JEWS.

Nazi hatred of Jews was partly based on traditional ANTISEMITISM. However, it also developed in its
own new direction, based on RACISM. This new antisemitism claimed that "Aryans" were biologically
superior to "parasitic Jews," who were racially inferior. Tremendous propaganda efforts reinforced
ideas such as these.

Hitler established the Reich Ministry of Public
Enlightenment and Propaganda on 5 March 1933,
with Goebbels at its head. The ministry used all
available means to communicate its message: party
rallies, parades, advertising, radio, films, theater,
and literature.

Radio broadcasts misinformed the German public during the war. It glorified German victories and
minimized German defeats. NAZI FILMS highlighted
the Nuremberg NAZI PARTY Rally in 1937, glorified
Germany as a dynamic world power, and promoted
antisemitism.

The Nazis gradually gained control over all newspapers. They distributed antisemitic literature, such
as *Der* STÜRMER. Time and time again they relied on
the basic belief behind their propaganda program:
"the great mass of people in the simplicity of their
hearts are more easily taken in by a big lie than by a
little one."

PROTOCOLS OF THE ELDERS OF ZION

Book which, for the past century, has been an influential antisemitic forgery. It tells of an imaginary
Jewish plot to take over the world.

The *Protocols of the Elders of Zion* is probably
the most widespread antisemitic myth in modern
times (see ANTISEMITISM). It was invented by agents of
the Russian secret police working in FRANCE during
the 1890s. It claims to show that the JEWS were ma-
nipulating events in all countries of the world in order to be able to control the world. In fact, it was
later shown that the work is an adaptation of an earlier work in which the villain was the French em-
peror, Napoleon III, and had nothing to do with Jews
at all. However, this was not known when the work
first appeared in Russia early in the twentieth century,
and was accepted as true by millions of readers.

The *Protocols* spread like wildfire all over the

German publication disseminating the "Protocols of the Elders of Zion" forgery

world. In GREAT BRITAIN and the United States, popular newspapers published excerpts from the "document." In 1920, the *Dearborn Independent*, the journal of the antisemitic car manufacturer Henry Ford, quoted selections from the *Protocols*. Ford did this to back up a series of articles that accused Jews of having influence in finance, the labor movement, and other areas of American life. In GERMANY, the *Protocols* also found a ready audience. By 1933, it had been through 33 editions there. To drum up popular support for their antisemitic programs, the Nazis and other racist organizations actively spread the lies found in the *Protocols*. They published it in many languages and had it distributed in many countries.

In the early 1920s, the *Protocols* were publicly shown to be a forgery. In 1921, *The Times* in London published a series of articles that showed its true origin. More details came to light during a trial held in 1934–1935 in SWITZERLAND. The trial exposed the links between this forgery and the Russian secret police. However, this did not stop the Nazis and other antisemites from continuing to publish and distribute the work.

Though long ago shown to be a forgery, the book continues to this day to circulate throughout the world and attract new audiences. Since it contains very few references to specific individuals or historical events, it can be manipulated to fit different situations and places.

Q U A K E R S

A religious organization dedicated to equality and humanitarian action. It is also known as the Religious Society of Friends. It was founded in the 1600s by the Englishman George Fox. Quakers share the belief that God is in the heart of the individual, regardless of race, creed, and gender. Currently, there are about 200,000 Quakers throughout the world.

After Adolf HITLER's rise to power, the European Quakers responded to "the cry of human suffering" caused by the Nazi regime. They were always careful to stay away from political disagreements and to remain unbiased within society.

Between 1938 and 1945, Nazis did not persecute German Quakers as they did other religious minorities. Quaker children were able to send packages to THERESIENSTADT and other GHETTOS. Later, they were allowed to send books and games to certain prisoners of war, provided that the material did not contain any handwriting or other form of "illegal communication."

Non-German Quaker organizations, such as *Le Secours Français* (French Assistance), participated in relief programs during the war. This included distributing food, clothing, and medicine to refugees. After the war, Quakers immediately set up relief organizations for German, Japanese, and Chinese civilians recovering from the destruction. (For Quakers in the United States, see AMERICAN FRIENDS SERVICE COMMITTEE.)

QUISLING, VIDKUN

(1887–1945) Fascist leader of NORWAY whose name became a synonym for treason. He served in various positions in the SOVIET UNION between 1918 and 1929. He decided that the greatest threats to the peace and stability of Norway were Bolshevism and communism. In 1931, he was a founding member of the Nordic Folk Awakening Party, (*Nordisk Folkereisning*), whose thinking was similar to that of the Nazis. That same year he became Minister of Defense. In 1933, he created an overtly fascist party, the National Unity Party, with its own youth movement, the "Hird." However, he failed to be elected to Parliament. He then turned to Nazi Germany and especially to its ideologist Alfred ROSENBERG. After WORLD WAR II broke out in 1939, Quisling revealed to the Nazi leaders his readiness to stage a coup and take power in Norway. He actively supported the German invasion of his country in 1940. Adolf HITLER rewarded him by appointing him premier of the government the Nazis set up after the invasion. The Germans, however, were soon disappointed in him. They dismissed him within a week. After that, the real power was held by the Germans, even though from 1942 Quisling held the title of Minister-President. Immediately after the liberation of Norway, Quisling was sentenced to death and executed for treason.

R A C I S M

Political program or philosophy based on ideas of race.

Racism assumes that cultural characteristics and differences in ability among individuals are determined by blood (race). This is usually coupled with a belief in the inborn superiority of a particular race and its right to dominate others.

From the second part of the nineteenth century, racial anthropologists—such as Houston Stewart Chamberlain—gave racism a false scientific backing. Chamberlain wrote that human history was a racial struggle, in which the Germans ("Aryans") were a superior race destined to rule over lesser ones.

This racism also held that a person's outward appearance revealed qualities such as intelligence and ability. Thus, "racial biology" involved noting physical measurements and descriptions to assign racial

values. A person's eye color, hair color, or head size and shape was carefully measured and recorded to determine racial inheritance.

Racism, especially racial ANTISEMITISM, was a central ingredient of Nazism. The 1935 NUREMBERG LAWS defined Jews by blood and not just by the religion they practiced or the community to which they belonged.

Today, the term racism is applied to many forms of prejudice and discrimination directed by one group against another. The evil example of Nazism is often quoted as a warning against such behavior.

Example of "Jewish Types" according to a German publication from 1938

Dr. Sophie Ehrhardt takes the "racial" measurements of a Gypsy woman in the Reich Health Office, Berlin

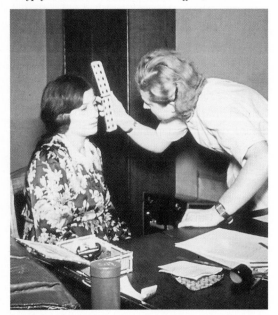

RAILWAYS, GERMAN

The railways of GERMANY (*Deutsche Reichsbahn*) and the Nazi-occupied countries, particularly POLAND, were a key element of the mass murders of the Holocaust. CONCENTRATION CAMPS and DEATH CAMPS were usually located close to railway lines. AUSCHWITZ-Birkenau, for example, was linked to almost every part of Europe by rail.

The Germans often imposed a special tax on the local Jewish community, which was used to help pay the costs of the DEPORTATIONS. Sometimes the deportees even had to pay for their tickets. Usually, deportees were transported in sealed cattle wagons, in which as many as 100 people (and sometimes even more) were crammed. The conditions during such journeys were inhuman. The victims often had no water and little food. A single bucket was provided for people to relieve themselves. Thus, many, especially those who were confined to the train cars for up to 10 days (such as the deportees from GREECE), did not survive the journey. Others lost their minds. This torment added to the sense of disorientation that the victims experienced upon arrival in Auschwitz and other camps. In order to preserve appearances, Jews from Germany and western European countries were sometimes sent in normal passenger trains, but these were also sealed and under heavy guard. Occasionally, people escaped from the trains, but the great majority of those who tried were killed in the attempt.

The movement of such large numbers of people, and the return of empty trains created a tremendous strain on the railway system. It was actually harmful to Germany's war effort, especially since it interfered with troop transports. Meetings were regularly held in Adolf EICHMANN's office in BERLIN in order to coordinate the movement of trains. The Germans found it necessary to increase greatly the number of railway workers.

Several million people were sent to their deaths through the offices of the *Deutsche Reichsbahn* and the local railways under its control. Railways were also used to move the possessions taken from Jews before their deportation and upon their arrival in the camps. After the war, none of the officials who organized the railways for deportations was put on trial.

Railway freight car used for deporting Jews, now in the US Holocaust Museum, Washington D.C.

Today, both YAD VASHEM and the UNITED STATES HOLOCAUST MEMORIAL MUSEUM in Washington have cattle cars that were used to deport Jews to camps on display to recall the role of the railways in the HOLOCAUST.

RAVENSBRÜCK

CONCENTRATION CAMP near Fierstenberg in eastern GERMANY. Ravensbrück was the only major camp created by the Nazis for WOMEN. The camp was opened in May 1939. It is estimated that 132,000 women of all European nationalities passed through the camp, and that 92,000 died. Ravensbrück had a training center for female SS guards. The camp had more female guards than any other camp. The commandants, however, were men.

The majority of prisoners were made to work in SS factories near the camp or in satellite camps, where private factories used their FORCED LABOR. Many of the women worked in the textile industry, producing SS uniforms and other garments for the Nazis. Conditions were extremely harsh. The women worked twelve-hour days and had to endure outdoor roll calls in all kinds of weather. The capacity of Ravensbrück was 15,000, but by 1944 it held over 40,000. In some huts six women shared one bunk. They received poor rations and were plagued by fleas and lice.

All women who were Jehovah's Witnesses and who were arrested by the Nazis were imprisoned in Ravensbrück. The camp also housed many political prisoners, including French resistance fighters. There were also Jewish prisoners. The Jews often received brutal treatment and were forced to do the hardest physical labor. A number of Gypsy women (see GYPSIES) were brought to the camp with their children in 1939. Other groups of CHILDREN arrived in the camp at various times. Over 800 children were born there during the period from 1943 to 1945. Most did not survive. In the summer of 1943, women began to arrive from AUSCHWITZ and other DEATH CAMPS and were joined by survivors from the WARSAW ghetto. At times, not all of the prisoners were women. In 1941, a sub-section of the camp was used to house male political prisoners. SOVIET PRISONERS OF WAR were also sent there beginning in 1942.

In the summer of 1942, cruel MEDICAL EXPERIMENTS began at Ravensbrück. Many Gypsy women were sterilized by Professor Carl Clauberg. Throughout 1942, transports of women from Ravensbrück were sent to death camps to be gassed. In late 1944, a GAS CHAMBER was installed in the camp and selections began (see SELEKTIONEN).

Ravensbrück was the center of a RESISTANCE move-ment since so many of the women were political prisoners. They managed to hold secret meetings and exchanged newspapers and war news. In 1944, many worked in armaments factories and were involved in sabotage.

Negotiations by the RED CROSS failed to stop the evacuation of the camp in 1945. At the end of March, thousands of starving women were forced on DEATH MARCHES to other camps in Germany. Many died on the way. On 30 April 1945, Soviet forces liberated the camp and found only 3,000 survivors.

RED CROSS, INTERNATIONAL COMMITTEE OF THE (ICRC)

International non-governmental humanitarian organization, which includes all national societies of the Red Cross and Red Crescent. Founded in 1863 by the Swiss Jean Henri Dunant, its headquarters are in Geneva. The ICRC's first legal framework was signed by 16 nations in 1864. Then, the organization's stated purpose was "for the betterment of the conditions of the wounded and sick in armed forces in the field." This was broadened in 1906 to cover war at sea. A third agreement, signed in 1929, extended the protection of international humanitarian law to prisoners of war. In 1934, a draft that would

Women prisoners in Ravenbrück at forced labor

have extended this protection to civilians in time of war, was agreed upon. However, the outbreak of WORLD WAR II prevented it from officially becoming an International Convention. The fourth Geneva Convention, protecting civilians in times of armed conflict, did not come into force until 1949, which was after the war had ended.

The absence of an ICRC Convention protecting civilians was the reason and excuse that the ICRC used for not acting on behalf of the millions of civilian victims of the Nazis during the war. It failed to condemn publicly the Nazis' appalling treatment of the Jews and to demand that the German government respect human rights. The ICRC argued that by trying to safeguard the rights of civilians it would risk losing its right to protect prisoners of war. No attempt was made to make the status of civilian prisoners equal to that of prisoners of war, which could have given them some protection. After a visit of its representatives to the THERESIENSTADT camp, the ICRC actually turned a blind eye to the terrible conditions and filed a favorable report about the "inspection." Nazi documents, discovered after the war, show that ICRC criticism could have had significant influence on Nazi behavior toward civilians.

Following the Allied Declaration of December 1942, concerning the massacre of JEWS, the ICRC un-

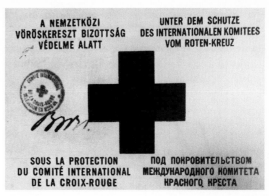

Sign at the entrance of a Jewish orphanage in Budapest, stating that the place is under the protection of the International Committee of the Red Cross

dertook some actions, but with little success. After the invasion of HUNGARY there was some ICRC intervention, chiefly by Friedrich Born, the ICRC representative in Hungary.

In general, activities such as these were not authorized by the executive of the ICRC itself. It was only at the commemoration of the 50th anniversary of the end of World War II in May 1995 that Cornelio Sommaruga, president of the ICRC, admitted the ICRC's "share in the responsibility for the total failure of a civilization that did not prevent the genocide of a people."

Red Cross nurses helping survivors in Vaihingen, Germany, 1945

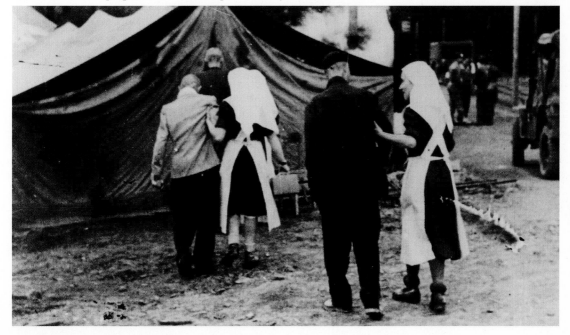

RED ORCHESTRA

Code name for one of the most successful spy networks of WORLD WAR II, which infiltrated the highest levels of German army intelligence. It was created by Leopold Trepper (1904–1982), who was born in POLAND and emigrated to PALESTINE in 1924. There he joined the Palestinian Communist Party, and was expelled by the British in 1929. He spent some years in Soviet Russia, and after the Nazis came to power he offered his services to the unit of the Red Army. In 1937, they sent him to western Europe, where, posing as a French Canadian businessman, he established a Russian spy network—which German counterintelligence called the Red Orchestra. It penetrated the highest ranks of the German air force and the German high command, sending invaluable information back to Moscow through its network of spies and radio operatives (know as "pianists").

Trepper received information from Jewish and communist informants at headquarters in Paris. In 1941, he provided Russia with advance information

Leopold Trepper, Head of the "Red Orchestra," in Belgium after the war

of the German attack. Joseph STALIN ignored the warning, saying that Trepper had been "intoxicated by English propaganda" and that there was no chance of a German attack before 1944. Toward the end of 1942, German counterintelligence closed in, destroyed the Paris bureau and arrested Trepper. However, he managed to escape and, in hiding, continued working through the French resistance.

After the war he returned to Russia but instead of a hero's welcome, was arrested and kept in jail for 10 years until after the death of Stalin. When he was released in 1955, he moved to Poland to be reunited with his family. He wanted to leave Poland because of antisemitism but was refused permission until 1973. He then returned to Israel, where he lived his remaining years.

REFUGEES

People fleeing from their homes and lands because of persecution or war.

The world has always had refugees. However, it was only after World War I (1914–1917) that protecting them was seen as an international legal obligation. Yet by the 1930s, many countries that had in the past been a haven for refugees had begun to enforce strict immigration controls, so as not to allow them in. Nevertheless, between 1933 and 1937, the guarantees provided by Jewish relief organizations allowed most of the refugees leaving Nazi GERMANY to be admitted to other countries in Europe, GREAT BRITAIN, PALESTINE (Israel), and North and South America.

In 1938, the persecution of Jews in Germany worsened. Following the German ANSCHLUSS with AUSTRIA in March 1938, a further 200,000 Jews came under Nazi rule. After KRISTALLNACHT (November 1938) and the occupation of CZECHOSLOVAKIA (March 1939), there were a further 150,000 refugees. A major refugee crisis was now at hand. Thousands of impoverished refugees fled to neighboring countries, or were forced to board ships without valid visas or landing permits.

The reaction of the nations of the world was to restrict immigration even more. One reason for this policy was the belief that loosening controls would encourage Germany to continue expelling its Jewish population. There was also the fear that eastern

European countries would follow Germany's example, adding millions of refugees to the existing crisis. For the Jews, the problem was even more serious, since the British had practically closed the doors of Palestine to Jewish immigration. The EVIAN CONFERENCE of July 1938, was unable to change the existing world climate of closed doors to refugees. By the beginning of WORLD WAR II in September 1939, some 350,000 refugees had escaped from Nazi Europe. Of these, 110,000 remained in European countries that fell into German hands in 1940.

As the German army advanced across Europe, 71,500 refugees were able to escape before borders were sealed in October 1941. Between 1940 and the end of the war, 90,000 refugees passed through Lisbon, PORTUGAL. The majority arrived after the fall of FRANCE in June 1940. In eastern Europe, 300,000 Polish Jews fled the German occupation into the Asian interior of SOVIET RUSSIA. Of the 2 million Jews under Soviet control, about 1.5 million managed to escape behind Soviet lines in the summer of 1941. During the war, small numbers of refugees continued to reach neutral countries, but wartime shipping problems made entry to these countries very complicated.

The Allies believed that the rescue of Jews could only be achieved by winning the war. This limited rescue attempts, such as the BERMUDA CONFERENCE in April 1943. It was not until the United States created the WAR REFUGEE BOARD, in January 1944, that a Government refugee body was established with the power to plan rescue operations, evacuate and care for refugees and negotiate with foreign governments. Although it succeeded in saving thousands of lives, the great majority of European Jewry had perished by this time. (See also DISPLACED PERSONS.)

REICHENAU, WALTER VON

(1884–1942) German army general and field marshal during WORLD WAR II. Reichenau was a supporter of Adolf HITLER. He became an army general in 1935. In 1939, he commanded an army in the German attack on POLAND and in 1940, he led an army in the western campaign. After the fall of FRANCE in June 1940, Reichenau became a field marshal.

When German forces invaded SOVIET RUSSIA in June

Polish Jewish refugees in Vienna after the war

1941, Reichenau led the troops that encircled KIEV in the UKRAINE. He issued an order calling for excessive cruelty toward SOVIET PRISONERS OF WAR and Soviet citizens, particularly JEWS. The order stated that German soldiers should inflict severe punishments on "subhumans"—Jews, according to Nazi views. Hitler recommended that all other army commanders issue similar orders.

In December 1941, Reichenau took command of Army Group South, operating in Russia. He died the following month.

REICHSSICHERHEITSHAUPTAMT

("RSHA")

Reich Security Main Office, which was formed on 27 September 1939, out of the previously existing Security Police, (SIPO). SIPO had been a combination of the GESTAPO, the Criminal Police and the SD (the Nazis' surveillance and intelligence force). Among its heads were Reinhard HEYDRICH (until his assassination) and Ernst KALTENBRUNNER. The RSHA became the most important Nazi terror organization.

During the war, the RSHA expanded its control over all policing and security work in the Reich, the occupied territories and directly behind the front line of military operations. In GERMANY, its planners were involved in shaping the planned postwar deportation and resettlement programs in Eastern Europe, known as GENERALPLAN OST. It also established and provided the manpower for the notorious EINSATZGRUPPEN killing units in POLAND and the SOVIET UNION. It went on to assume a major role in planning and carrying out the murder of the JEWS throughout occupied Europe. In particular, Adolf EICHMANN, as head of Subsection IV B-4 of the RSHA, was responsible for the DEPORTATIONS of the Jews of Europe to the DEATH CAMPS in Poland.

R E I C H S T A G

GERMANY's parliament from 1871 to 1945. Under the democratic Weimar Constitution of Germany's WEIMAR REPUBLIC (which lasted from 1919 to 1933), the Reichstag was elected every four years, by all the people, by secret and direct vote. In theory, the parliament was the authority of the state, since all governments were formed with its approval. In practice,

however, the Reichstag during the Weimar Republic had two fatal faults. First, the German president had the right to dissolve the Reichstag. Second, its election law allowed parties with very small support to be represented in parliament. An increasing number of small parties were appearing in the Reichstag in the late 1920s. It became more and more difficult to form a government that could bring together a majority of the votes. By 1930, the Reichstag was not highly regarded among the people. The president governed largely by himself, issuing emergency decrees. The shortcomings of the Weimar government were emphasized by the growth of right-wing parties, including Adolf HITLER's National Socialists.

The Nazis came to power in January 1933, although they were still a minority. They did not receive a majority of votes in the election or a majority of seats in the Reichstag. Even so, Hitler was asked to form a government. He did so with the help of smaller conservative parties. In order to achieve more popular support in the country, the Nazis organized a fire that burned down the Reich-

Russian soldiers raise the Soviet flag over of the bombed ruins of the Reichstag in Berlin, 1945

stag building in BERLIN on 27 February 1933. They accused their communist opponents of starting the blaze and pretended that the fire was meant as the signal for a communist uprising. They then staged a big show trial of communist leaders and outlawed the Communist Party.

On 23 March 1933, less than two months after Hitler was inaugurated as chancellor, the Reichstag gave up its authority. After that, the parliament existed as a one-party legislature until 1942, but had no legislative powers.

REICHSVERTRETUNG DER DEUTSCHEN JUDEN

("Reich Representation of German Jews")

Organization representing the JEWS in Nazi GERMANY.

The Reichsvertretung was established on 17 September 1933, after the Nazi rise to power. Under the leadership of Rabbi Leo BAECK, with Otto HIRSCH as its executive director, it included the regional organizations of the country's Jewish communities and most of the major Jewish associations. A few right-wing German-Jewish organizations refused to join. Some associations of German Orthodox Jews entered the Reichsvertretung only in July 1938.

After the NUREMBERG LAWS, in September 1935, the organization lost its voluntary status and had to change its name to Reichsvertretung der Juden in Deutschland ("Reich Representation of Jews in Germany"). This was because the Nazis denied that the Jews were German. It was made compulsory for all German Jews to be members of the organization by February 1939. A decree of 4 July 1939 officially recognized the organiztion and placed it under the supervision of the Interior Ministry. The main tasks of this unified body—besides political representation—were to organize emigration, welfare activities, and educational work. German authorities saw an advantage in dealing with a single centralized Jewish organization, which was supervised by the RSHA (see REICHSSICHERHEITSHAUPTAMT), in carrying out their anti-Jewish policy. While the Jewish communities were charged with informing those chosen for DEPORTATION and providing them with supplies, there is no evidence that the leadership of the Reichsvertretung played any direct part in organizing the mass deportations of 1941 and onward. The organization

was dissolved on 10 June 1943. Most of its leaders perished in the HOLOCAUST.

RELIEF AND RESCUE COMMITTEE OF BUDAPEST

(*"Va'adat ha-Ezra ve-ha-Hatzala be-Budapest"*)

Committee established early in 1942 to assist Jewish REFUGEES, who had been pouring into HUNGARY. They had been coming from GERMANY since 1933 and from AUSTRIA since 1938. Their presence in BUDAPEST created a financial burden on the community, which tried to look after their welfare. Leading figures in the Budapest Jewish community volunteered to raise funds for this purpose. This became more difficult with the arrival of even more refugees from Germany, the former CZECHOSLOVAKIA, POLAND, and YUGOSLAVIA. Most all of them had crossed the border illegally. If they were caught, they were imprisoned. The Budapest community tried to "legalize" the presence of the refugees by providing them with forged papers or by bribing clerks in the Home Office. By 1943, the situation had become critical and a Zionist Rescue Committee was formed, which worked with the existing one. The Committee also worked together with other Jewish rescue groups and representatives in SLOVAKIA, Istanbul and SWITZERLAND.

The aims of the Committee were to rescue JEWS from neighboring countries, legally or illegally; to aid the refugees; and to prepare for the self-defense of Hungarian Jewry. The field work was carried out by some 400 Zionists, mostly members of youth movements. In the spring of 1944, the Committee reported that there were some 18,000 refugees in Budapest. They were supported partly by the community and partly by funds received secretly from abroad.

The Committee took on a significant amount of rescue work. When it heard of the possibility of a "deal" with the Germans to win freedom for some Jews, it entered negotiations. As a result, 1,700 Jews were allowed to depart for Switzerland; while 20,000 were deported to the concentration camp of STUTTHOF instead of being sent to the death camp at AUSCHWITZ. The Committee made contacts with the neutral powers, the Vatican, and the RED CROSS to get them to intervene on behalf of the Hungarian Jewry. It organized illegal emigration via ROMANIA and

Some of the 1,700 Hungarian Jews allowed to leave Hungary for Switzerland in 1944

distributed forged papers. It also convinced foreign diplomats to supply protective passports to some 80,000 Jews in Budapest.

REPARATIONS AND RESTITUTION

Financial repayment and compensation. Even before the end of WORLD WAR II, and before the extent of Jewish suffering became clear, Jewish organizations (notably the WORLD JEWISH CONGRESS) raised the question of reparations for Jewish survivors and restitution for Jewish holdings that had been robbed by the Nazis. At the end of the war, the Jewish world had to aid and resettle hundreds of thousands of penniless survivors, who wished to rebuild their lives in PALESTINE and elsewhere. The JEWISH AGENCY sent a letter to the four allied powers (the UNITED STATES, GREAT BRITAIN, FRANCE, and SOVIET RUSSIA) demanding that a portion of German wealth be set aside to settle Jewish claims for reparations. However, the matter was not treated as urgent.

Jews rejected the idea that they could in any way be compensated for the suffering to which they had been subjected. Even so, many felt that the Germans should be forced to participate in, and per-

haps even fully finance, the cost of resettling the survivors. There was also a desire to see GERMANY provide reimbursement for the tremendous amount of Jewish property stolen by the Nazis for which there were no heirs. Moreover, the new-born State of ISRAEL, which was absorbing thousands of survivors, required enormous financial support. At the same time, the birth of the Federal Republic of Germany brought with it the rapid rebuilding of the West German economy.

In 1951, Israel presented a claim to the four allied powers. Shortly after, German Chancellor Konrad Adenauer announced that he was willing to negotiate with representatives of Israel and diaspora Jewry about German compensation. In Israel and the Jewish world, however, there was considerable debate about the ethics of such an arrangement. There were many people who believed that there should be no dealings of any kind with the Germans and that agreeing to accept money was like selling the souls of the victims. Among the strongest opponents was Menachem Begin, then Israel's opposition leader. He denounced the talks and led angry demonstrations against them. The Israel parliament, however, voted in favor of reaching an agreement with the Germans by a very small majority.

The Conference of Jewish Material Claims Against Germany was established to represent the claims of individuals. Nahum Goldmann (who headed both the World Jewish Congress and the World Zionist Organization) was its chairman. That body joined the Government of Israel in negotiations with the West German government. In September 1952, the Luxembourg Agreement was concluded. West Germany committed itself to aiding Israel in the amount of $845 million over a period of 14 years. Much of that aid was to take the form of German industrial goods, including merchant ships, railway carriages, and electric equipment to help Israel's economy. In addition, individuals, German Jews especially, were able to receive compensation for the property that they had been forced to abandon, careers that had been interrupted, and suffering in CONCENTRATION CAMPS and GHETTOS. Much of that money was distributed in the form of pensions. Over the course of the last 40 years, this has amounted to billions of dollars paid out by West Germany, which has fully observed its commitments in the agreement.

However, Jews who remained in countries behind the Iron Curtain received nothing. Jews from countries other than Germany were not compensated at the same level as German Jews. East Germany denied all responsibility for the HOLOCAUST and rejected claims that it too should bear a part of the costs of Jewish rehabilitation (restoration). In many instances, East Germany even refused to process the application of those who had difficulty in documenting their claims. AUSTRIA negotiated a separate arrangement, but refused to take responsibility for the claims of non-Austrian Jews who suffered in Austria.

In recent years, with the collapse of communism, Jews have made claims for property stolen in Eastern Europe. In 1992, the World Jewish Restitution Organization (WJRO) was established to coordinate these efforts. The organization has also taken steps to retrieve the Swiss bank accounts of Jews killed in the Holocaust, as well as money and valuables taken from Jews and deposited by Nazis in SWITZERLAND.

The WJRO has also worked to secure the return of Jewish property robbed in Norway and other countries. Laws concerning the return of Jewish property have been passed in a number of countries, notably SLOVAKIA and HUNGARY. The German government has been pressed to extend its compensation payments to include impoverished survivors in former communist countries.

RESCUE COMMITTEE IN TURKEY AND GENEVA

see JEWISH AGENCY.

RESCUE OF CHILDREN

Even before the outbreak of WORLD WAR II, efforts were being made to rescue Jewish CHILDREN who had come under Nazi rule. Most of those who worked to get Jewish children out of Europe were Jewish groups.

One of the first efforts was YOUTH ALIYA, which took children to PALESTINE. Youth Aliya workers continued their work, even during the war (see TEHERAN CHILDREN). Ten thousand children reached Britain in the KINDERTRANSPORTS. Several hundred were taken to the United States by the German Children's Jewish Aid, established in New York in 1934.

Once war broke out, plans to save individual children were often made by parents on an informal basis. In eastern Europe many children were successfully smuggled out of GHETTOS and hidden in non-Jewish districts. Sometimes Jewish parents paid money to individuals living outside the ghettos who promised to look after their children for the duration of the war.

The majority of Jewish children rescued during the HOLOCAUST were saved as a result of these personal arrangements. Rescue on a larger scale was attempted by various organizations and networks that were established during the war. The Council for Aid to Jews (ZEGOTA) was an important rescue body run by non-Jews. It was first founded in WARSAW, and later opened branches in other Polish towns. It aimed to provide aid to JEWS living in non-Jewish areas and to provide forged documents for Jews in hiding. In July 1943, a special department for children was established. It worked to place Jewish children in family homes or institutions. In all, 2,500 children came under the care of Zegota in Warsaw.

An UNDERGROUND program of child rescue was organized in FRANCE. It was coordinated by the Jewish health society, OSE. When the DEPORTATION of Jews started in France in 1942, many local organizations participated in the rescue of Jewish children. For this effort, Catholic and Protestant Church leaders (see CHRISTIAN CHURCHES), peasants, and underground groups all joined together under the leadership of George Garel. They rescued children from internment CAMPS and placed them in Christian homes and institutions. They provided the children with aid and false papers. From 1942 to 1944, many Jewish children were smuggled to safety over the borders of SWITZERLAND and SPAIN. It is estimated that 7,000 children were saved in France. RESISTANCE movements in the NETHERLANDS and BELGIUM were also successful in rescuing thousands of children by hiding them in boarding schools, hospitals, and monasteries.

It was very difficult for parents to part with their children. They feared that the children might be orphaned, baptized as Christians, or turned in to Nazi authorities by false rescuers. The motivations of the majority of rescuers, however, were genuine. They acted on humanitarian principles, out of a deep moral conviction, or because of political views (see "RIGHTEOUS AMONG THE NATIONS"). Hiding a Jewish child was considered by the Nazis as a crime punishable by death.

Many difficulties faced those involved in rescuing children. Rescued children often had to live in hiding so they would not cause suspicion. For example, boys who were circumcised, children who could not speak the local language, and those without forged documents were at risk of being found out.

Resistance and rescue organizations worked hard to produce documentation that would keep a child safe, especially birth certificates showing a new name and a Christian religion. On one hand, the children themselves were very confused and unhappy to be separated from their families. They needed help to adjust to their new environment

---

The Jewish Council in Amsterdam, created in February 1941, had to work for the Nazis.... The Nazis needed the committee to register the Jews [before the deportations]. The committee also included Jewish people working with the Dutch underground.... One asked if I would like to work with him, and said, "We are going to try to save the children from transport."

[Among the empty buildings in the old Jewish quarter] there was a theater [which the Nazis used to collect Jews for deportation]. Across from the theater was a Jewish orphanage. We were assigned by the Germans, two women and eight men, a group of ten, to live in the orphanage. Our duty was to register the infants in the theater, take the children away from the parents into that orphanage. We had to clean them up, we had to put fresh diapers on them, and wrap them up in blankets, and bring them back to the theater for transport.

The Nazis didn't realize that after we took the children back into the big [theater] hall where their parents were, we had a different exit. We knew exactly the whole layout of the theater, and we went out the other way, got back to the orphanage, and that was it. A truck picked up those children.... They were accompanied by the driver and maybe one or two other men or women—non-Jewish—and they went into the country. They delivered the children to the farmers, mostly farmers, and gave them special ration cards...and they kept the children. And this was going on every night for quite a while. At times, we could get a bigger child in between.... The parents were sent away without the children. We did not inform the parents of what we did, because we were afraid that they might talk.

From the testimony of Molly Hertzfeld, Gratz College Oral History Archives.

I was selected for this particular camp in Sudeten Deutschland, southern Germany, to manufacture the V-2 missiles [rockets shot by the Germans at London] from September 1944 until liberation, 9 May 1945. There were so many different operations and hundreds of screws. You have to make the hole, drill the hole half the size of this screw in order to keep it in. Then I got the idea that it's time to do something. We didn't have any arms, we didn't have resistance. Let me do it my way. I made larger holes for the screws figuring that they wouldn't hold. I shortened the screws to a half. If they had been magicians, they could not find out once you put the screw into the hole.

I wasn't satisfied with doing it myself. I wanted Germans to do the same thing. I was on good terms with the German mechanics working alongside each other in the factory. I asked each of them separately, "How are you doing this? Don't you have any cramps in your palms? Don't tell the next guy, don't tell anybody. I'm going to give you an easier way of doing it." And I told them that bigger holes made it easier—and I got the whole crew doing the same thing.

There was a lull. The V-2 bombs stopped coming into Great Britain, and were blowing up on the launching pad in Germany. A commission came and started to investigate. They found little things but they couldn't possibly check out whether the holes were the proper size. It gave me so much pleasure that I didn't care if they shot me or not.

From the testimony of Anatole Gorko, Gratz College Holocaust Oral History Archives

and to learn their newly created life histories. On the other hand, many established close links with their new families. Problems sometimes arose after the war (SEE FOSTER HOMES). It was always easy to find and identify Jewish children who had been sheltered in Christian institutions so they could be brought back to a Jewish environment.

RESISTANCE, JEWISH

Physical and spiritual means employed by Jews to defend themselves against the Nazis. After the war, many people asked why the Jews went to their deaths seemingly without a struggle, "like sheep to the slaughter." In fact, Jews fought in many different ways, in GHETTOS and CAMPS, and as PARTISANS, against the humiliation forced upon them by the Nazis.

It is important to remember the situation of the Jews during the HOLOCAUST when considering the level of Jewish resistance. There was little that Jewish leaders could do without leading to deadly reprisals against the whole community. Jewish leaders who refused to follow Nazi orders were killed. Jewish communities were isolated from one another and received little moral or practical support

from local populations. Furthermore, they were weakened by starvation and deprivation. Finally, the unbelievable nature of the situation in which they found themselves prevented action. It was difficult to accept that the Nazis planned the murder of a whole people.

Non-military forms of defiance were common in the ghettos and camps. Jews resisted Nazi laws by smuggling food for their survival. They observed religious and national traditions (see JEWISH RELIGIOUS LIFE DURING THE HOLOCAUST), established schools, youth groups, and underground newspapers. They encouraged cultural activities in order to maintain their dignity and boost morale.

In general, the JUDENRAT (Jewish Council) leaders felt that cooperating with the Germans would save lives. They argued against resistance. Some Jews, mostly young people, decided that armed resistance was necessary, although they recognized that they could do very little real harm to the Nazis. Some joined partisans in the forests; others stayed in the ghettos, helping to smuggle in weapons. There were several armed Jewish revolts in the ghettos. The most famous was the WARSAW GHETTO UPRISING, led by a JEWISH FIGHTING ORGANIZATION established in 1942. On 19 April 1943, 2,000 Germans entered the ghetto in tanks, intending to destroy it. Jewish fighters were waiting in hiding and forced the tanks to retreat. The whole ghetto resisted: those with weapons fought and others hid and refused to surrender. Many held out until May. There were also other ghetto revolts. Examples include BIALYSTOK in August 1943 and VILNA, in September 1943. After these uprisings, many Jews escaped to the forests to continue fighting as partisans. In MINSK, the Judenrat was involved in resistance and helped over 6,000 people escape from the ghetto.

Large numbers of Jews were involved in partisan activities in eastern Europe, while others fought with Tito's partisans (see YUGOSLAVIA) and in SLOVAKIA. In western Europe, Jews participated in the UNDERGROUND resistance in FRANCE and to a lesser extent in BELGIUM.

In the camps, although people were starving and dying, some still physically resisted. Members of the SONDERKOMMANDO planned uprisings in SOBIBÓR, TREBLINKA, and AUSCHWITZ-Birkenau. In October 1944, Jews attacked the SS and succeeded in setting fire to a crematorium (see GAS CHAMBERS, GAS VANS, AND CREMATORIA) in Birkenau. Most were shot as a consequence. Jews were involved in many acts of resistance in the CONCENTRATION CAMPS and LABOR CAMPS, including many acts of smuggling and sabotage.

R H O D E S

Greek island in the Mediterranean Sea. In 1912, Rhodes came under Italian rule. Some 5,000 JEWS lived there at the time. When new antisemitic measures were passed by the Italian government in 1938, Jewish families that had arrived after World War I were expelled, and more than half the local Jewish population decided to leave the island. Many settled in central Africa.

In September 1943, Rhodes was occupied by German troops. By July 1944, all the remaining Jews—numbering 1,700—had been rounded up and sent to GREECE. There they were held in jail and then deported to the DEATH CAMP at AUSCHWITZ. By the end of the war, only 161 survived.

RIBBENTROP, JOACHIM VON

(1893–1946) Nazi GERMANY's foreign minister (1938–1945). He joined the NAZI PARTY in 1932. As ambassador-at-large he negotiated the Anglo-German Naval Agreement in 1935 and the anti-Comintern "Rome-Berlin-Toyko" Axis in 1936. From 1936 to 1938 he was ambassador to GREAT BRITAIN. There his odd social behavior, such as greeting the king with a Nazi salute, attracted attention. During his stay in London he became increasingly anti-British.

"Illegal" immigrants to Palestine whose boat had sunk reaching the coast of Rhodes in 1939

Joachim von Ribbentrop

After years as an outspoken anti-communist, Foreign Minister Ribbentrop signed the NAZI-SOVIET PACT on 23 August 1939.

The Pact guaranteed 10 years of non-aggression between Germany and the SOVIET UNION. By December 1940, however, Adolf HITLER was already planning his attack on Russia, and Ribbentrop began losing influence. Seeking to win back Hitler's favor, he pressured German allies and satellite states to push ahead with the DEPORTATION of the local Jewish populations. In April 1943, he told Admiral Miklós HORTHY of HUNGARY to either kill the Jewish population or send them to CONCENTRATION CAMPS. "There is no other possibility," he insisted.

After the war, Ribbentrop was sentenced to death (see TRIALS OF WAR CRIMINALS) and hanged.

RIEFENSTAHL, LENI

(1902–) German PROPAGANDA film maker. Riefenstahl became a well-known film actress and documentary film director in the late 1920s.

Riefenstahl's fame comes from the propaganda films that she created, for the Nazis. Her most famous work, *Triumph of the Will*, recorded and glorified the 1934 Nuremberg Reich Party Day Rally. Her film made a powerful impression on German and international audiences. It emphasized the orderliness, unity, and power of the new government. She followed this with a film about GERMANY's military rearmament. Riefenstahl was assigned to capture the 1936 OLYMPIC GAMES on film. The result was the two-part film *Olympia*.

Leni Riedenstahl (dressed in white, foreground) filming a Nazi movie at the 1936 Olympic Games

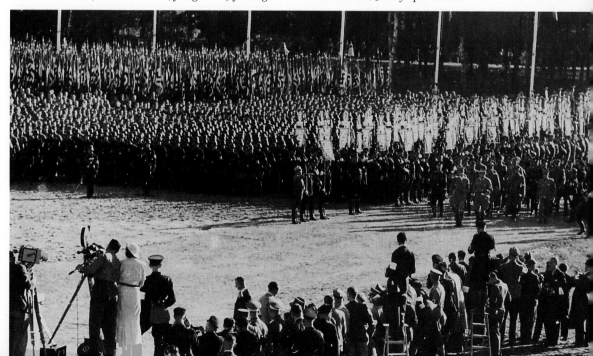

RIEGNER CABLE (TELEGRAM)

The first documented evidence of the "FINAL SOLUTION" to reach the west.

Dr. Gerhart Riegner was the WORLD JEWISH CONGRESS's chief officer in Geneva. In mid-1942, he was contacted by a successful German businessman who wished to pass information on to the Allies. Eduard Schulte, whose name was released only decades later, informed Riegner that the most senior Nazis had decided upon the complete slaughter of the JEWS of Europe and that a form of poison gas would be used for this purpose.

On 8 August 1942, Riegner sent the information by telegram to key contacts: Rabbi Stephen S. WISE in the United States and Sidney Silverman, a Member of Parliament in London. The telegram to Wise was sent via the United States State Department. The State Department withheld the telegram from Wise, perhaps fearing that the information could

The Riegner Cable bringing the first information on the Nazi extermination of Europe as conveyed by Sidney Silverman of the World Jewish Congress in London to Rabbi Stephen S. Wise in New York

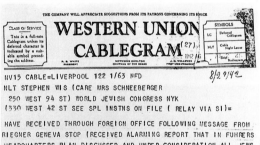

damage the Allies' war effort. Silverman, who had received his telegram from the British Foreign Office, informed Wise of the telegram's existence. Then, Wise directly approached the Secretary of State, demanding action.

The United States government refused to allow the information to be released publicly until the Nazis' intention to exterminate the Jews could be confirmed by other sources. The American representatives in Switzerland were charged with confirming Riegner's findings. Between August and November, they collected four written statements that proved that Schulte had told Riegner the truth. The evidence that the State Department found most convincing was that of Dr. Carl J. Burckhardt of the International RED CROSS.

On 17 December 1942, as a result of the Riegner Cable, the Allies made a joint statement called the "German Policy of Extinction of the Jewish Race," which declared that those involved in such crimes would not escape punishment. This was the first commitment to pursue, prosecute, and punish war criminals.

United States Secretary of Treasury Henry J. MORGENTHAU, Jr., later wrote: "We knew in Washington, from August 1942 on, that the Nazis were planning to exterminate all the Jews of Europe." The original of the Riegner Cable is now in the UNITED STATES HOLOCAUST MEMORIAL MUSEUM in Washington.

R   I   G   A

Capital of LATVIA. In 1935, the Jewish population of Riga numbered 43,000 and it was the cultural center of Latvian Jewry. In June 1940, it was annexed, with the rest of Latvia, to SOVIET RUSSIA. The Germans occupied Riga on 1 July 1941, 10 days after they attacked Soviet Russia. Even before their arrival, Latvians were spontaneously attacking Jews.

Nazi persecution of Riga's Jews began immediately with the occupation. At first, pogroms were organized by the EINSATZGRUPPEN, involving volunteer units from the local population. Restrictive laws imposed on the Jewish community stripped them of their possessions and mobility. Ritual slaughter for kosher food was prohibited. Jews could purchase food in only three stores and even that food was rationed restrictively. In the fall of 1941, a GHETTO

German soldiers welcomed by the local inhabitants on their arrival in Riga, 1941

was created and more than 30,000 inhabitants were forced within its walls. On 19 November 1941, the Germans divided the ghetto into a "small" and "large" ghetto. Working Jews were segregated into the small ghetto. On 30 November, known as "Bloody Sunday," more than 10,600 Jews were marched out to nearby Rumbula Forest and murdered. A second *aktion* (operation) on 8 December claimed a similar number of victims. Estimates of the total number of victims in this period approach 28,000.

In the months that followed, Jews from within Germany were deported to the Riga ghetto. By this time, the ghetto was reorganized, with a JUDENRAT in charge. Group and individual murders continued through the fall of 1943. Finally, on 2 November 1942, all the old, very young, and sick residents of the Riga ghetto were murdered. The remaining residents were transferred to the Kaiserwald CONCENTRATION CAMP, which had been established in Latvia. When the Soviet army liberated Riga on 13 October 1944, only about 150 Jewish survivors came out of their hiding places.

There was an active UNDERGROUND in the Riga ghetto, with 200 to 300 members. In October 1942, anticipating a general evacuation order, a small number of fighters attempted to join up with PARTISANS operating in the area. They were ambushed

and most were killed in the fighting. Several days later, in a typical Nazi action of reproach, over 100 Jews were murdered along with the entire ghetto police force.

"RIGHTEOUS AMONG THE NATIONS"

Title given to non-Jews who risked their lives to save JEWS during the HOLOCAUST. The title comes from the phrase in the Talmud: "The righteous among the nations of the world have a place in the world to come."

Since 1962, a Commission for the Designation of the Righteous, headed by an Israeli Supreme Court justice, has worked under the YAD VASHEM Remembrance Authority in Jerusalem. This committee is in charge of awarding the title. In order to make the award, the committee examines the deeds and motivations of the rescuer.

Among the many questions the committee asks are: 1) Was the rescuer paid? 2) What were the dangers and risks faced by the rescuer at the time? 3) What were the rescuer's motivations? Was it friendship, religious belief, etc.? 4) What is the evidence provided by the rescued person or his/her representative?

The "Righteous Among the Nations" boulevard at Yad Vashem, Jerusalem

A serious candidate for recognition as a "Righteous among the Nations" would be a non-Jewish person who risked his or her life, freedom, and safety in order to rescue one or more Jews from the threat of death or DEPORTATION, without asking for payment.

One interesting problem that has come before the committee involves the question of danger. Technically, those who helped Jews risked their own lives and those of their families, since this was against Nazi law. However, diplomats enjoyed immunity from prosecution in the countries in which they were serving. Aristides de SOUSA MENDES, the Portuguese consul in FRANCE, Sempo SUGIHARA, the Japanese consul in KOVNO, and Paul GRÜNINGER, the Swiss police captain on the Austrian border, all aided many Jews. Although they were not in actual danger, de Sousa Mendes and Grüninger lost their jobs and suffered considerable hardship. In each case the committee chose to honor them.

There are several cases in which groups aided Jews in making their way to safety. The Danes were successful in transporting more than 7,000 Jewish residents to SWEDEN. The story of the Dutch village of Nieuwlande is impressive in a different way. There, in 1942 and 1943, it was agreed that each household would hide one Jewish family or at least one Jew. The danger was equally shared by all the members of the community, and there was no chance of denunciation to the Nazis since all were involved. Every villager was recognized as a "Righteous among the Nations." The small French town of LE CHAMBON-SUR-LIGNON saved thousands of Jews, and its leaders were honored.

It is estimated that between 10,000 and 20,000 rescuers could qualify for official recognition by Yad Vashem. As of the end of 1994, nearly 12,000 men and women received the honor. They prove that it was possible, even in the darkest of times, to come to the rescue of their fellow men. The rescuers' heroism is especially praiseworthy when one thinks of the enormous numbers of people throughout the countries of Europe who watched silently as their neighbors were deported to the DEATH CAMPS or even participated in the crimes.

Psychologists have recently begun to study the rescuers in order to learn what led them to do what they did. The difficult decision to risk oneself and one's family came from a combination of several factors: altruism (willingness to give for others), a strong sense of morality, a personal relationship with the rescued person, political convictions, religious convictions, the belief that he or she was

NOTED "RIGHTEOUS AMONG THE NATIONS"

BENOÎT, MARIE French Catholic monk who helped Jews escape from France to other countries.

DUCKWITZ, GEORG FERDINAND German diplomat who was sent as maritime attaché to occupied Denmark and was instrumental in saving Dutch Jewry from the Holocaust.

FRY, VARIAN American volunteer in France who forged many documents to save the lives of many Jews.

GRÄBE, HERMANN German who employed many Jews under the Nazis' forced labor but aided them instead of abusing them.

HAUTVAL, ADELAIDE French physician who managed to save the lives of infected women and kept it a secret in the Auschwitz concentration camp and also protested the mistreatment of Jews.

KARSKI, JAN Polish official who brought news of the plight of Jews in Germany and Poland.

LUTZ, CARL Swiss diplomat who managed to supply passports to thousands of Jews wishing to emigrate to Palestine from Budapest.

SCHINDLER, OSKAR Czech businessman who helped thousands of Jews from the Plaszów camp by employing them in his factory, thus saving them from the horrible conditions in the camp. He kept a list of all the workers, which became known as "Schindler's List."

WALLENBERG, RAOUL Swedish diplomat who used unusual methods in rescuing Jews in Hungary and Germany. He issued passports stamped with the Swedish seal. He also worked with the Jews in helping them establish hospitals, soup kitchens and nurseries.

WESTERWEEL, JOOP Non-Jewish Dutch teacher who became involved in establishing an underground movement for young Zionist pioneers. The pioneers were put into hiding and then he helped them escape from Nazi-occupied Europe.

---

competent enough to succeed with the rescue. At least one of these factors has been found in the rescuers. It has also been learned that once a person became involved in rescuing Jews, he or she tended to become more active in further rescues rather than less active. The well-known story of Oskar SCHINDLER's "List" reflects a complex person whose commitment to rescuing grew once he began the process.

RINGELBLUM, EMANUEL

(1900–1944) Jewish historian and founder of the Oneg Shabbat Archives of the WARSAW ghetto. By

1939, Ringelblum was a noted historian in Warsaw who had published many scholarly works on the history of Polish Jewry.

Ringelblum also served as a staff member of the AMERICAN JEWISH JOINT DISTRIBUTION COMMITTEE (JDC) in POLAND. He went with other JDC officials in October 1938 to the border town of Zbaszyn. They were trying to help the thousands of Polish JEWS who had been expelled from Nazi GERMANY, but were not allowed by the Poles to enter Poland.

After the German invasion of Poland in September 1939, he continued to work with the JDC. They established welfare programs and soup kitchens for those in need. However, his greatest achievement serve—for future generations—a complete and objective history of Jewish life in Warsaw during those horrible years. They wrote detailed articles on selected topics, towns, and villages. He collected interviews and DIARIES from the ghetto's inhabitants. He documented the economic, political, and cultural life in the GHETTO and compiled information for the RESISTANCE. Ringelblum and his colleagues composed reports on the systematic mass murder of the Polish Jews. Some of these reports were then smuggled out of the country by the Polish UNDERGROUND and used to expose Nazi crimes to the world.

To preserve this material, the Oneg Shabbat Archives were buried in tightly sealed milk cans and other containers, in two locations in the ghetto. In 1946 and 1950, the materials in one location were uncovered. Those hidden at the other site, however, have never been found. The Oneg Shabbat Archives are now housed with the Jewish Historical Institute in Warsaw.

Ringelblum himself died in the HOLOCAUST. In March 1943, he and his family left the ghetto and went into hiding on the non-Jewish side of Warsaw. In March 1944, their hiding place was discovered. Ringelblum, his family and the other Jews found hiding in the secret bunker were taken to the Warsaw ghetto, then in ruins, and executed.

To this day, the Oneg Shabbat Archives remain one of the most valuable sources of information on Jewish life in German-occupied Poland.

Cases being brought out of the rubble of the Warsaw Ghetto containing the Ringelblum Archives

of the war period was in creating the Oneg Shabbat Archives of the Warsaw ghetto. *Oneg Shabbat* means "Sabbath pleasure" and is used for cultural gatherings on Saturday afternoons. The group responsible for the archives used to meet secretly on Saturday afternoons.

In October 1939, Ringelblum began collecting information during the day and compiling notes on this data at night. This was risky work, since preserving such records was forbidden by the Nazis. Within months, he had found a few dedicated individuals to work with him. By May 1940, it became a large project, which eventually involved the work of dozens of other people.

Ringelblum and his associates wanted to pre-

ROHM, ERNST

(1887–1934) Nazi leader. Ernst Röhm was a long time ally of Adolf HITLER and a key figure in Nazi politics. He joined the German Workers' Party (the forerunner of the Nazi Party) before Hitler, in 1919, and the SA upon its founding in 1921. Following the 1923 Beer Hall Putsch in Munich, Röhm, like Hitler, was found guilty of treason, but he was discharged on the same day that he was sentenced.

Despite the close personal friendship between the two, Röhm's release from prison led to his first disagreement with Hitler. Following the unsuccessful Munich coup, Hitler began calling for the patient use of legal means in order to seize power. Röhm, on the other hand, believed that the SA should form the basis of a reconstituted German army, which

Ernst Röhm (center of first row) with members of the SA. in Munich, 1932

would seize power by force. He assumed the leadership of the SA in 1924, but because of his disputes with Hitler, he resigned this position the following year, as well as all other posts in the Nazi Party.

In 1929, Röhm settled in Bolivia, but Hitler summoned him back to Germany in 1930 and charged him with rebuilding the SA. His organizational skills were remarkable: the SA grew from 70,000 to over 4.5 million members in just four years. With the rise of the Nazis to power in 1933, Röhm became minister without portfolio in Hitler's cabinet and minister of the Bavarian local government. Most leading Nazis, however, despised the obese, openly homosexual Röhm. Industrialist supporters of the regime resented his continued calls for a socialist revolution, and the military feared that he would create a *Soldatenstaat* (soldier state) with himself as chief military commander. Even Hitler was wary of Röhm, who openly discussed sharing power with the FÜHRER.

With Röhm and his SA men threatening the stability of the Nazi regime, Hitler finally summoned him for a showdown. They sat together for five hours, and eventually decided that the SA would take a one-month vacation, during which time they would be forbidden to wear their uniforms. However, on the night of 30 June 1934, Röhm was arrested. A gun was left in his prison cell but Röhm refused to commit suicide. "If I am to be killed," he said, "let Adolf do it himself." According to witnesses, two ss officers then shot him. About 70 other Nazi leaders and many civilians and SA members were also killed in the purge, known as the "Night of the Long Knives."

R O M A N I A

Central European country that was made up of the union of Walachia and Moldavia in 1859. After World War I, Romania grew considerably by annexing Northern TRANSYLVANIA, BUKOVINA, BESSARABIA and Dobruja. The percentage of JEWS in these areas was very high—sometimes as much as 30 percent (as compared to 4 percent in the country as a whole). There were nearly 800,000 Jews in Romania on the eve of WORLD WAR II. It was the third largest Jewish community in Europe, after POLAND and SOVIET RUSSIA. Jews made an important impact on the life of the country. This was true despite ever-growing ANTI-SEMITISM and the creation of openly antisemitic political parties, such as the National Christian Defense League and the IRON GUARD. The short-lived government of Octavian GOGA in 1937–1938 introduced a

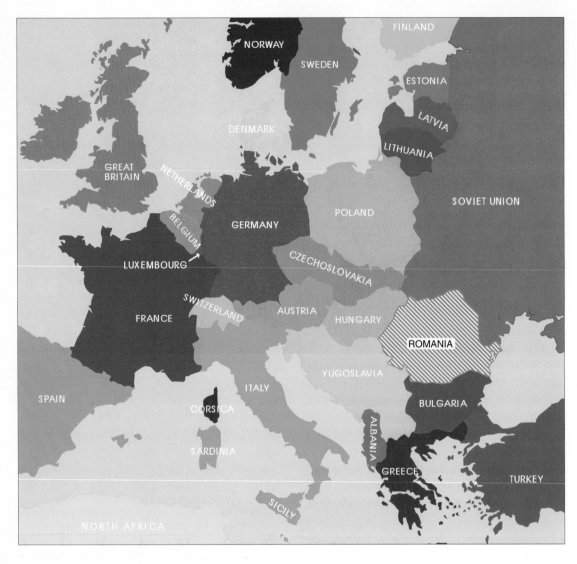

series of particularly tough anti-Jewish measures.

Romania was very weak when World War II broke out. Although the country allied itself to GERMANY, it lost some of its newly acquired territories. Northern Transylvania was given to HUNGARY, and its entire Jewish population was eventually deported to AUSCHWITZ. Northern Bukovina and Bessarabia were given to SOVIET RUSSIA and southern Dobruja to BULGARIA. A deeply humiliated country took out its anger on the Jews. Romanian troops in the town of Dorohoi massacred 200 Jews. The pro-German government of Ion ANTONESCU was established in September 1940. It adopted a number of harsh measures, which led to mass looting of Jewish property. Jews were excluded from commercial life and lost the right to vote. Only those who had obtained Ro-

manian citizenship before August 1916 were allowed to keep it. The government seized 40,000 Jewish homes and handed them over to non-Jews. Jews were subject to FORCED LABOR in special camps. A number of POGROMS broke out, like that of Iasi (JASSY) in June 1941, which left over 10,000 Jewish dead. Jewish organizations, represented by community head Wilhelm Filderman and Chief Rabbi Safran, managed to keep channels of communication open with the authorities and saved what could be saved. Adolf HITLER intended the "FINAL SOLUTION" to be implemented in Romania, but by that time, the tide of war was turning against the Germans and Antonescu resisted. However, when the lost provinces of Bukovina and Bessarabia were reconquered by the Romanian army, the Jews of these

Improvised hospital for the wounded inside the synagogue in Bucharest after the pogrom of 23 January 1941

areas were accused of collaboration with the Soviet Union. They were declared an "enemy population" by Antonescu. An estimated 150,000 Jews were massacred in those provinces and the survivors deported to TRANSNISTRIA.

Throughout the war, Romania was used as an escape route by Jews fleeing the HOLOCAUST. An estimated 5,000 sailed from the Black Sea port of Constanta with the hope of reaching PALESTINE (see STRUMA and MAURITIUS).

When the war ended, only 400,000 Jews were left in the country. In many cases, they did not get their houses or property back. Their citizenship, however, was restored. Two-thirds of the 350,000 Romanian Jews who died in the Holocaust were killed not by the Germans, but by the Romanians and Hungarians.

R O M E

Capital of ITALY. Rome was the home of Europe's oldest Jewish community. It has existed for 2,000 years. When WORLD WAR II broke out, the community numbered over 12,000. In 1938, the Fascist government of Benito MUSSOLINI (see FASCISM AND FASCIST MOVEMENTS) introduced ANTI-JEWISH LEGISLATION to the country. Many leading Roman Jews were expelled from professions, the universities, businesses, schools, and social life.

Even after Italy entered World War II in June 1940, life in Rome's Jewish community went on as usual. Although more antisemitic laws were passed in 1941, Roman police remained unwilling to arrest JEWS for violating them. This all changed with the arrival of the Germans.

At first, Rome's Jews were, joyful about the fall of Mussolini's government in July 1943. However, the new government under Marshal Pietro Badoglio did little to improve their lives. The racial laws were left in place. Disaster struck in September when the Badoglio government was overthrown by German forces who took over the country and entered Rome. Lists of Jews living in Rome fell into German hands. This allowed the GESTAPO to find and arrest Jews.

Herbert Kappler was the head of Rome's Gestapo office. On 25 September 1943, he received orders from Heinrich HIMMLER that "all Jews, regardless of nationality, age, sex, and personal conditions, be transferred to GERMANY and liquidated." Instead of carrying out the operation immediately, he chose to first confiscate 50 kilograms/110 pounds of gold from the Jewish community. Adolf EICHMANN sent his representative, SS Captain Theodor Dannecker, and a special group of 44 men to Rome to reinforce Himmler's order. The first raid in Rome came suddenly in the early morning of 16 October 1943. Dannecker's men, aided by Italian police, arrested every Jew they could find, regardless of age, sex, or nationality. By the end of the day, they had seized over 1,200 people. The prisoners were deported to AUSCHWITZ two days later. Dannecker proudly reported these numbers to Himmler. However, the truth was that the vast majority of Roman Jews had managed to escape. Many had foreseen the coming Nazi raid and made arrangements to hide among the Italian population. Others hid in Rome's many churches and monasteries.

Dannecker's failure to round up a greater num-

Monument at the Ardeatine Caves, Rome, scene of a massacre by the Germans of non-Jewish and Jewish Roman citizens, March 1944

ber of Jews led Himmler to replace him with Friedrich Bosshammer in January 1944. Bosshammer was under pressure from BERLIN to get results. He, in turn, pressured the Italian police to find and arrest Jews. He offered rewards for turning in Jews, and organized bands of informers to expose those in hiding. Even so, his success was very limited.

During the Ardeatine Caves massacre, the last few months of the German occupation, Bosshammer's men committed one of the worst atrocities in the history of the war in Italy . The killing on 23 March 1944 of 33 German police by Italian resistance forces led Bosshammer to order a reprisal action. Ten civilians would be executed for every German killed. On the next day, SS detachments collected 335 captives from the Regina Coeli prison, including 77 Jews, and transported them to a nearby ancient Christian burial cave. Here they systematically shot each person in the back of the head. They then sealed the cave and left the bodies to be found after the Germans left the city.

When the American army arrived on 4 June 1944, thousands of Roman Jews finally came out of hiding. They had been saved by a sympathetic population whose refusal to cooperate was greater than the pressure the SS could put on them.

Today, the Ardeatine Caves are a site of pilgrimage with a monument commemorating the massacre.

ROOSEVELT, FRANKLIN D.

(1882–1945) President of the United States, 1933–1945. When Franklin Roosevelt became president his main concern was ending the Great Depression which had ruined the American economy. Millions of people were jobless and banks, businesses, and industries were failing. He created welfare programs to assist struggling Americans. For this he won the affection of many American JEWS. They supported him throughout his presidency despite his failure to try to save Jews from Europe. Today some people believe American Jews were naive to support Roosevelt. Other contend that Roosevelt's inactivity notwithstanding, the Republican alternatives would have been worse.

Roosevelt's REFUGEE/rescue policies must be analyzed in both a domestic and foreign policy context. Believing that immigrants would take away jobs

President Franklin D. Roosevelt at his White House desk , Washington D.C., 1933

from American citizens. Americans were vehemently anti-immigration. They ignored the fact that immigrants could create jobs, particularly if they came as a family unit which many Jews did. Anytime Roosevelt allowed more refugees to enter he was criticized by anti-immigrating forces. Roosevelt did not alter the policy introduced by President Hoover. This permitted American officials to refuse a visa to any immigrant who fulfilled all other legal requirements, if the official believed the immigrant might eventually need public assistance. Numerous American consular officials used this clause to keep Jews out.

Roosevelt generally adopted a "do as little as is necessary" policy when it came to aiding Jews. He made some weak attempts to assist. After the ANSCHLUSS he convened the EVIAN CONFERENCE in 1938. Similarly in 1943 he convened the BERMUDA CONFERENCE. Both were supposed to come up with rescue alternatives but failed to accomplish much. Finally in 1944 when he learned that the State Department had actively sabotaged efforts to rescue Jews, he created the WAR REFUGEE BOARD. It came too late to have a real impact.

Some claim Roosevelt did not want to rescue Jews. Evidence does not bear this out. Beset by many other problems, he failed to consider rescuing Jews a priority. By the time the Nazis' intentions became clear it was too late to do much. Though he could not have rescued all European Jewry, many more people could have found refuge in the United States if the president had recognized the importance of this effort.

ROSENBERG, ALFRED

(1893–1946) Nazi ideologist and Minister for the Eastern Occupied Territories (1941–1943). He was an early NAZI PARTY member and Adolf HITLER entrusted him with leading the party while Hitler was imprisoned following the unsuccessful Beer Hall Putsch in 1923 (see RÖHM, ERNST). Rosenberg impressed Hitler with his pseudo-scientific racial theories and his antisemitism.

Rosenberg's book, *The Myth of the Twentieth Century*, appeared in 1930. It was a best-seller, second only to Hitler's MEIN KAMPF. In the work, he blamed Christianity for allowing the JEWS to take hold of the world. He called for the abandonment of the Old Testament (the Hebrew Bible). In its place should be substituted Nordic sagas and fairy tales, so that the heritage of the Jews would not be respected. He saw all history in terms of racial conflict.

Alfred Rosenberg (left) reviewing troops in Kiev

In 1934, he became the head of the Center for Nazi Studies. He was responsible for documenting and sorting through the great Jewish archives of Europe. In the process, he destroyed and looted many of them (see EINSATZSTAB ROSENBERG). Many of these books and documents which were not "selected" to be saved were sold by the ton for scrap. As Minister for the Eastern Occupied Territories, he oversaw all the orders for continuing to GHETTO and deporting of Jews, and confiscating their property.

Rosenberg was found guilty of crimes against humanity at the TRIALS FOR WAR CRIMINALS at Nuremberg and hanged.

R   S   H   A

see REICHSSICHERHEITSHAUPTAMT.

R U B L E E   P L A N

Offer made by GERMANY in 1938 to permit the mass emigration of Jews from Germany in return for great amounts of money for the THIRD REICH. It was made, with Adolf HITLER's permission, by Hjalmar SCHACHT, president of the Bank of Germany. He made the offer to George Rublee, an American lawyer whom President Franklin D. ROOSEVELT had appointed director of the Intergovernmental Committee for REFUGEES.

The Germans were in a difficult economic situation. They proposed to release 50,000 Jewish workers each year over the next three years in return for $1.2 billion. The Jews would not be allowed to take their belongings and would have to leave their families behind as hostages. United States Secretary of State Sumner Welles and many (but not all) Jewish organizations and leaders opposed this solution to the refugee problem. They claimed it "rewarded Germany for robbery and expulsion." Negotiations for setting the scheme in motion in a modified form continued into 1939. The plan had to be dropped when war broke out in September 1939.

RUMKOWSKI, MORDECHAI CHAIM

(1877–1944) Head of the JUDENRAT in the LÓDZ ghetto. In the eyes of historians, Rumkowski was the most controversial of all the leaders of the

Jewish councils in the GHETTOS throughout POLAND.

After an unsuccessful career in business, Rumkowski became director of a Jewish orphanage in a suburb of Lódz. He entered Jewish politics and was a member of the Jewish community board in Lódz. After the German invasion of Poland in 1939, Rumkowski was named head of the Jewish Council (the Judenrat). As such, he faced the problem of all Judenrat leaders. He had to run a government in the ghetto that could provide food, shelter, heat, medicine, and work to a starving population, with few resources. His only power came from his German masters.

The German occupation force was particularly harsh in its treatment of the Lódz Jews. In addition to demanding FORCED LABOR and confiscating Jewish property, the Germans blew up synagogues. When the ghetto was sealed in April 1940, 164,000 Jews lived in 48,100 rooms, most of them without running water or sewer connections.

The Lódz ghetto, unlike the one in WARSAW, could be cut off from the outside world both above and below ground. Unlike in Warsaw, the Lódz Judenrat controlled all aspects of food, work, and shelter. Rumkowski ran the ghetto like a dictatorship. The Judenrat controlled everything—hospitals, dispensaries, schools, orphanages, even a thriving cultural life. When rabbis were no longer allowed to work, Rumkowski himself performed marriages. His picture appeared on ghetto currency.

He developed what he believed to be a long-term strategy for survival—salvation through work. He

Mordechai Chaim Rumkowski stamp issued in the Lódz Ghetto with textile workers in the background

was determined to save the Jews of Lódz by making them a productive and indispensable work force for the Nazis.

Conditions worsened when 20,000 Jews from GERMANY, LUXEMBOURG, and CZECHOSLOVAKIA were brought into the ghetto. Five thousand GYPSIES were also imprisoned in one section.

Yet, despite its impressive productivity and the profits made by ghetto industries, the Nazis were not content to let Lódz remain a working ghetto. During the first five months of 1942, 55,000 Jews and all 5,000 Gypsies were deported and murdered in GAS VANS at the CHELMNO DEATH CAMP.

In early September 1942, the Nazis demanded that all children and old people be deported. Rumkowski obeyed. "The decree cannot be revoked. It can only be slightly lessened by our carrying it out calmly," he said. In a public speech, he pleaded: "Brothers and sisters, hand them over to me. Fathers and mothers, give me your children."

Rumkowski was consistent. "I must cut off the limbs to save the body itself," he argued. "I must take the CHILDREN because if not, others will be taken as well." In the next 10 days, 20,000 children and old people were deported to the Chelmno death camp.

For a while, it seemed that Rumkowski's strategy had worked. During the period between September 1942 and May 1944, when the other ghettos of Poland were being emptied, Lódz was spared.

But even Lódz did not escape the "FINAL SOLUTION." On 23 June 1944, deportations to Chelmno resumed and other groups were sent to AUSCHWITZ. Even then, Rumkowski pleaded with the Jews to go to the trains in an orderly fashion. Those who came voluntarily could bring luggage, those who did not would be rounded up by the Jewish police.

Of the Lódz Jews, 60,000 died in the ghetto and 130,000 were deported to death camps.

Rumkowski himself was deported in August 1944 to Auschwitz, where he was murdered. Some say he died at the hands of Jews. Others hold that he was treated as any other old man and selected for gassing.

R U S S I A

see SOVIET RUSSIA.

SA ("Sturmabteilung")

"Storm Troopers" or "Brownshirts"; Adolf HITLER's fighting wing during his campaign for power in GERMANY.

The idea and the first actual experiment in organizing a revolutionary street army came from Captain Ernst RÖHM. The SA was organized in 1922, supposedly for the purpose of protecting party meetings. In fact it was intended as the army of a Nazi revolution. Hitler used the SA as a threat, blackmailing his opponents into giving him access to power when the right moment would arise. It served as a source of propaganda against the WEIMAR REPUBLIC, which he claimed was a "Jewish disgrace to German dignity."

With the economic crisis of the early 1930s, the SA appealed to jobless youngsters as well as many farmers and lower-middle-class Germans unwanted by both the left and the traditional right. It gave them a routine to follow, street fights to be engaged in, dead heroes to worship and a venomous antisemitism to practice. Many joined the SA with the simple aim of gaining a material reward once Hitler would come to power. They believed that they would be repaid with jobs, commissions, and access to the property of the rich and the Jews.

In April 1931, Hitler made himself the supreme commander of the SA. Under Röhm, the organization grew in power. Its influence increased in the period prior to Hitler's appointment as Reich Chancellor on 30 January 1933. Estimates of its size vary from 800,000 to 2 million. When Hitler came to power, the SA assumed an official character, joining the regular police in fighting communists. The last free elections in Germany, early in March 1933, were subjected to SA terror. Illegal CONCENTRATION

SA troops marching in Coburg, Germany

CAMPS, erected by local SA units, sprang up all over Germany. However, policy differences between Röhm and Hitler developed. The army and the SS were also jealous of the power of the SA, which led Heinrich HIMMLER to caution Hitler that Röhm was plotting against him. On 30 June 1934, known as the "Night of the Long Knives," Röhm and most of the regional SA leadership were accused of treachery and murdered by the SS. Afterwards, however, the SA was reorganized and continued to play an important role in the Nazi system. It provided military training for hundreds of thousands of Germans, guarded concentration camps and committed innumerable cruelties.

S A C H S E N H A U S E N

CONCENTRATION CAMP in Oranienburg, 20 miles north of BERLIN, GERMANY. The camp was established in September 1936. It was used as a training ground for SS junior officers and leaders, who were then sent to other CAMPS to work. It held many different kinds of inmates, including criminals, GYPSIES, Jehovah's Witnesses, HOMOSEXUALS, and political prisoners. After KRISTALLNACHT in November 1938, some 1,800 Jews were sent there and many were murdered. Prison-

ers had to wear different colored BADGES depending on their status. For example, homosexuals wore a pink triangle and Jews a yellow star.

After the war broke out in 1939, Polish and SO-VIET PRISONERS OF WAR were also sent to Sachsenhausen. Over 13,000 were shot. Later, a GAS CHAMBER was installed. Conditions in the camp worsened during the war. Overcrowding became a real problem. The camp was built to hold 10,000, but by April 1945, it held over 50,000. Jewish prisoners were housed in separate barracks and treated with brutality. Notable prisoners, such as Pastor Martin NIEMÖLLER, were also housed in separate barracks.

Cruel MEDICAL EXPERIMENTS were carried out on Gypsies, Jews and homosexuals. Dr. Werner Fischer performed experiments that tried to show that Gypsies had blood that was different from "Aryans." He only succeeded in causing a great deal of suffering. Many people were murdered for these experiments. Often, their skeletons and organs were sent to German universities to be used in research.

Sachsenhausen had 61 sub-camps, where slave laborers worked long hours for various private German firms. One of the harshest working environments was a large brick factory near the camp. Most prisoners in the later stages of the war were used

Prisoner parade in Sachsenhausen

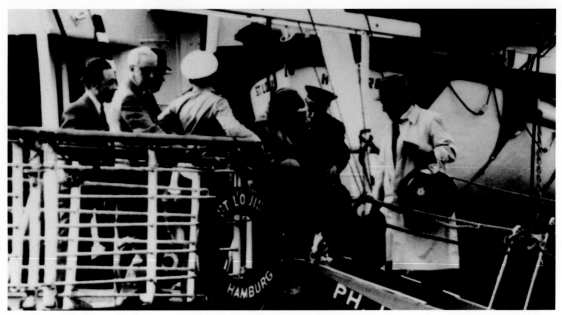

The "Saint Louis" in Antwerp

for FORCED LABOR to increase armaments production. Many were worked to death.

On 2 February 1945, the RED CROSS visited the camp and offered to take it over. The Nazis refused to agree to the plan. Instead, the prisoners were forced on a DEATH MARCH through Germany. They died in large numbers of hunger and exhaustion.

Sachsenhausen was liberated by Soviet soldiers on 27 April 1945. At that time, only 3,000 very sick inmates remained. It is estimated that a total of 200,000 prisoners passed through Sachsenhausen.

Much of the camp is still preserved, including the site of the medical experiments. It includes a museum and a memorial at its center.

"SAINT LOUIS"

German luxury liner that carried more than 900 Jewish REFUGEES holding Cuban landing permits from GERMANY to Cuba. They arrived just before the war, but were not permitted to land.

On 13 May 1939, the *Saint Louis* set sail from HAMBURG with 937 passengers destined for Cuba. The majority were JEWS, who had purchased landing permits from corrupt Cuban officials so that they could leave Nazi Germany. Over 700 of these were on the list for UNITED STATES immigration quotas. Unknown to the ship's passengers or its captain, Gustav Schroeder, the

Cuban president, Federico Laredo Brú, had declared all permits and visas issued before 5 May 1939 to be invalid. Cuban public opinion was strongly influenced by local antisemitic press campaigns and German PROPAGANDA. Most Cubans were not sympathetic to the problems of the refugees.

When Brú learned that the *Saint Louis* and two other ships carrying Jewish refugees were on their way to Cuba, he ordered immigration officials to keep the passengers from leaving the ship. On 27 May 1939, the *Saint Louis* arrived in Havana harbor. Cuban authorities allowed only 22 passengers with valid visas to go ashore. The others were forbidden to leave the ship.

While the passengers on the *Saint Louis* anxiously waited on the ship, officials from the AMERICAN JEWISH JOINT DISTRIBUTION COMMITTEE (JDC) tried to negotiate with Cuban leaders. The negotiations failed. On 2 June, Brú ordered the Cuban navy to escort the ship outside the country's territorial limits. Appeals for action were made to Western leaders, such as British Premier Neville Chamberlain and United States President Franklin D. ROOSEVELT, as well as the United States Congress. These appeals were ignored. Leaving Cuban waters, the ship slowly sailed close to the shore of Florida, hoping that United States officials would grant the passengers refuge. However, the *Saint Louis* could not get permission to land in the United States. It began its return trip to Europe. After a month at sea, passengers learned that the Belgian, Dutch, French, and British governments had agreed to take in 214, 181, 224, and 287 refugees respectively.

Most of the former *Saint Louis* passengers who landed in BELGIUM, the NETHERLANDS, and FRANCE perished during the Holocaust. They were trapped in those countries after the Germans invaded. In 1976, the story of the *Saint Louis* was told in the movie, *The Voyage of the Damned*.

S A L O N I K A

Port city on the northeastern mainland of GREECE.

For centuries Salonika was one of the greatest centers of Sephardi Jewish religion, scholarship, and culture.

Greece was invaded by the Nazis in April 1941. The city's Jewish population of over 50,000 came under direct German rule. The Nazis immediately destroyed synagogues, arrested the Jewish community's leaders, banned all Jewish newspapers, and seized the contents of the city's Jewish libraries. On Saturday, 7 July 1942, all Jewish men were forced to assemble in the city's central square for registration. They were subjected to public humiliation before the spectators. Nine thousand Jewish men were forced to do hard labor during 1942. In December, the community's cemetery was raided and the tombstones used for paving roads and building latrines.

Salonika's JEWS were the first to be deported as a group from Greece. Chief Rabbi Zvi Koretz was chosen in December 1942 to be the community's leader and go-between with the Nazis. He adopted the approach of obeying the Germans in an attempt to reduce their hostility. This decision had the tragic result of making the murderous work of the Nazis easier. In early 1943, SS officers Alois BRUNNER and Dieter WISLICENY were sent to Salonika by Adolf EICHMANN. These men, aided by the German foreign office's Maximilian Merton, were in charge of the DEPORTATION of the city's Jews. They completed this task with remarkable speed.

The city's Jews were forced into GHETTOS, beginning in February 1943. They were required to wear yellow BADGES and register their property. They were forbidden to use facilities such as public transportation and telephones.

The Nazis' plan was to deport the community section by section. In March 1943, they informed Rabbi Koretz that one section of the ghetto, the Baron de Hirsch quarter, was being relocated to

Deportation of Jews from Salonika, 1943

Monuments in Salonika cemetry to Salonikan Jews perished in the Holocaust

KRAKÓW, POLAND. The Nazis promised him that the people would be welcomed and looked after by the Kraków Jewish community. Each person could pack a limited amount of luggage. All were sent directly to AUSCHWITZ. This pattern of "relocation" continued for three months, with up to 2,500 Jews deported on some days. By May 1943, 46,000 Jews had been sent from Salonika, mostly to Auschwitz where they were gassed on arrival.

For Salonika's Jews, there was little hope of refuge. A handful of Jews were hidden. The government of ITALY used its diplomatic representatives to save a few hundred Jews. The Italians took advantage of the Nazis' official definition of Jews for deportation, which excluded Jews who held non-Greek nationality. Italian diplomats prevented the deportation of 281 Jews with Italian citizenship, and made sure that another 48 who had lost their citizenship were able to regain it. When the threat to the Jews became more serious, the Italians arranged for Jews to be smuggled into Italian-occupied Greece. The governments of SPAIN and Turkey took similar action to save the lives of some of Salonika's Jews.

After the war, between 1,300 and 2,000 Salonikan Jews returned to the city. They found that only two of their nineteen synagogues were still standing and that their cemetery had been turned into a quarry (it later became the site for a university). The issue of the property stolen from deported Jews is still unsettled. Alois Brunner escaped from Europe and settled in Syria. Dieter Wisliceny was tried and executed in SLOVAKIA in 1948.

SAUCKEL, FRITZ

(1894–1946) Prominent Nazi. Sauckel was a member of the Nazi Party from 1923 and the Nazi leader of Thuringia in Eastern Germany from 1927 to the end of the WORLD WAR II.

Until 1942 he was a rather unimportant figure. However, after the winter of 1941–1942, which was an economic disaster for Germany, he was given full control over Deployment of Labor in the Reich. As such, his main task was to organize the DEPORTATION of millions of people from the occupied areas to work as FORCED LABOR in the German armaments industry.

Sauckel was sentenced to death at the TRIALS OF WAR CRIMINALS at Nuremberg and was hanged in October 1946.

SCHACHT, HJALMAR

(1877–1970) German economist and president of the German State Bank (Reichsbank).

Schacht was first appointed president of the Reichsbank in the 1920s, but resigned in March 1930. Although he did not join the NAZI PARTY, he believed that Adolf HITLER's policies could bring economic stability to GERMANY. Hitler thought that Schacht was a financial genius and reappointed him Reichsbank president in March 1933.

In 1934, Schacht became the economics minister. He worked to strengthen the German economy and promote rearmament.

Schacht resigned from his post as economics minister in November 1937. This was partly because he disagreed with the idea of neglecting all economic areas except preparation for war. He remained in the cabinet until 1943.

Since he had loose ties with RESISTANCE circles, he was imprisoned after the July 1944 attempt to assassinate Hitler (SEE PLOT TO KILL HITLER). At the NUREMBERG TRIAL, Schacht was found innocent of war crimes charges. He wrote two accounts of his years in office, both translated into English: *Account Settled* and *Confessions of the Old Wizard*. After the war, he rebuilt his banking business and died a wealthy man.

SCHINDLER, OSKAR

(1908–1974) Businessman whose activities in saving JEWS during the HOLOCAUST were brought to the attention of millions in Steven Spielberg's award-winning movie, *Schindler's List*.

Oskar Schindler was born in Sudetenland, CZECHSOLOVAKIA in 1908. He took over two factories, which had previously been owned by Jews in POLAND following the German invasion there in 1939. The two factories, were very successful, and he established a third factory producing kitchen enamels near KRAKÓW. During this time, he witnessed the growing mistreatment of Jews during the German occupation of Poland. The liquidation of the Kraków

ghetto in 1943 had a tremendous affect on him. He employed Jews from the nearby PLASZÓW labor camp in his factory in order to rescue them from the brutal conditions in the camp.

When the Russian army advanced into Poland in October 1944, Schindler re-established his factory, which by then was no longer in use, in Brunnlitz, Sudetenland. Schindler was able to use his connections to move Jewish workers to his factory, thereby saving their lives. The names of these workers' were written down on a list, now better known as "Schindler's list." During this time, Schindler also managed to rescue additional Jewish prisoners from the GROSS-ROSEN CONCENTRATION CAMP as well as 300 women sent to AUSCHWITZ. Schindler, aided by his wife, took special pains to ensure that his workers were treated well, giving them food and medical care.

Schindler's efforts saved about 1,100 Jews. After the war, he lived in difficult circumstances but received some support from those he had rescued. He died in Germany but was buried in a Christian

Oskar Schindler (left) at his Emalia factory in Zablocie, an area of Kraków

Early in 1949, a group of Jews saved by Schindler gathered privately at an Alsatian restaurant in Paris, to celebrate with their friend Oskar Schindler (second from right), who was passing through the city

cemetery in Jerusalem. At YAD VASHEM, the Holocaust museum in Jerusalem, he planted his own tree in

SD in Antwerp

the Garden of the Righteous in recognition of his humanitarian actions.

The power of Oskar Schindler's story was clearly shown in *Schindler's List*, which was based on a book by the Australian author, Thomas Keneally. Filmed in a black-and-white format to give it a realistic, documentary effect, *Schindler's List* tells the story of one man's transformation from an ordinary person with many failings into a modern day hero.

SD (Sicherheitsdienst)

("Security Service")

(1931–1945) Security Service of the SS and the intelligence gathering agency of the NAZI PARTY.

The SD was established as a party organization under Reinhard HEYDRICH in 1931. After the Nazis came to power in 1933, the SD also took on government responsibilities. Its main task was to set up and maintain a broad spy network among the German people. It made security reports on the state of public opinion and on the activities of supposed political and "racial" enemies of the Nazi regime. It also reported on the political loyalty of institutions, organizations, and even individuals. Military intelligence, the ABWEHR, also came under the rule of the SD in 1944.

The SD had its own anti-Jewish section and played an important role in the HOLOCAUST. German police officials in the occupied eastern territories, and EINSATZGRUPPEN (mobile killing unit) officers, were frequently higher SD officials.

After WORLD WAR II, the International Military Tribunal at Nuremberg (see TRIALS OF WAR CRIMINALS) declared the SD a criminal organization. Its members were subject to arrest, trial, and punishment as war criminals.

"Selection" on arrival in Auschwitz

S E L E K T I O N E N

("Selection")

When used by the Nazis, the term selection meant the sorting of prisoners or deportees into two groups—those judged able to work and those who were to be killed.

At AUSCHWITZ, selections often occurred when a transport arrived. Those considered unable to work, especially CHILDREN, the elderly, and women with small children, were taken directly to the GAS CHAMBERS. Others were admitted to the camp. From time to time, prisoners in the camp underwent further selections. In the GHETTOS, selections were also used to choose JEWS for DEPORTATION.

S E L F - H E L P

Welfare, religious, educational, and cultural organizations that operated in GHETTO society, but which were not officially permitted. Unlike the JUDENRAT, Jewish councils that were set up by the Germans, these alternative organizations were often secret. Participation was voluntary and they were supported freely by those involved.

Women and children selected for death in Auschwitz

When the Nazis invaded POLAND in 1939, the Jewish population began to suffer. Organizations came into being which helped with the basic needs of survival under the harsh conditions. Such organizations and committees provided shelter, first aid, fire protection, food, and medical services. This network of organizations came under the control of a Coordinating Commission, and later, an independent body, the ZSS (Jewish Communal Self-Help). Following the German occupation, the ZSS had some measure of official approval beginning in May 1940. By early 1942, the ZSS had 412 branches. In mid-1942, it was dissolved by the Germans. Its founder and head was Michael Weichert. Under his leadership the ZSS's basic strategy was to rescue what could be rescued. It provided food for CHILDREN and the sick, distributed clothing, medicine, and money, and operated orphanages. At its largest, the ZSS (called ZTOS in WARSAW) was similar to the Judenrat in size and scope. However, the relationship between the Judenrat and the ZSS was sometimes strained.

It is estimated that more than 50 percent of the eastern European Jewish population was religiously observant. The Sabbath and Jewish dietary laws (kosher food) were widely adhered to. The demand to continue the basic institutions of religious Jewish life was strong, even under the horrible conditions in the ghettos. In every ghetto, secret prayer services were held, ritual slaughter of meat was practised whenever possible, matzah was baked for Passover, and ritual baths were used. All this was done secretly, and often at the risk of personal safety. The secret organizations that served religious needs are another important part of the Self-Help network (see JEWISH RELIGIOUS LIFE IN THE HOLOCAUST).

The Germans closed down Jewish schools. This had the effect of forcing community education UNDERGROUND. Informal gatherings of students took place all over Poland. When the Germans finally allowed Jewish councils to run elementary and vocational schools, these informal gatherings became the basis for the official schools. Schools of various types were operated throughout the ghettos.

Boredom and despair were among the horrors of ghetto life. With little to do and increasing challenges to daily survival, the Jews turned to entertainment to raise their spirits. Cultural pursuits and informal entertainment were, by late 1940, organized by the ZTOS entertainment committee in Warsaw. Yiddish theater, ghetto orchestras, and lectures entertained ghetto residents. Lending libraries were established, the largest being in the VILNA ghetto. The library there contained 100,000 books. The historian Emanuel RINGELBLUM set up a secret Jewish archive in the Warsaw ghetto. It gathered materials that described and recorded the destruction of the communities. Other archives were established in LÓDZ, Vilna and BIALYSTOK. These efforts inspired many Jews in the ghettos of Europe to record their experiences.

This vast network of welfare, religious, educational, and cultural organizations served community needs under shocking conditions. They document the struggle within the ghetto to maintain—as much as possible—all aspects of a dignified life.

S E R B I A

Region of YUGOSLAVIA. Sixteen thousand JEWS lived there before the Nazi occupation.

In April 1941, GERMANY rapidly conquered Serbia. Within a month, the new military government had imposed a full range of anti-Jewish laws. Jews had to register all their property, wear the yellow BADGE, and suffer economic deprivation. In July 1941, Jewish property was "Aryanized" (see ARYANIZATION). One month later, Jewish men were sent to FORCED LABOR camps. Within a very short time period, the authorities had enacted laws that Germany itself had taken eight years to set into motion.

PARTISAN attacks on the Nazis in Serbia began soon after the Nazi occupation. The mountainous Serbian terrain and dense forests gave the partisans advantages that the Nazis could not overcome. Jews identified strongly with the partisans and many joined their ranks. Serbia's Jews were often blamed for the activities of the Serbian partisan networks—the communists and the royalist CHETNIKS—who continually assaulted the Germans.

In June 1941, a member of the Zionist youth movement Ha-Shomer ha-Tzair set fire to a military truck in Belgrade. In response, all Belgrade's adult male Jewish population was ordered to assemble in a city square. One hundred of these men were selected and held as hostages for information about the location of the person responsible. When no information was forwarded, these men were shot.

This method of holding civilians responsible for partisan attacks became the pattern for Nazi-Jewish relations in Serbia. Jewish support for partisans served as the Nazis' justification for quickly "solving" the Jewish "problem." The Nazis tried to stop partisan activity by severely punishing civilians after each incident.

In October 1941, while Nazi decision makers were planning a way to speed up the destruction of Serbian Jewry, a partisan group attacked a German army unit in Topola and killed 21 soldiers. In return, the military commander ordered the shooting of 2,100 Jews and Gypsies, who were being held in LABOR CAMPS. One hundred inmates were murdered for each German soldier killed. From this point onward, the Nazis declared that in response to any partisan action, 100 Jews, GYPSIES or communists would be shot for each soldier killed. Fifty would be killed for each soldier injured.

Over just a few months, 4,000 to 5,000 Jewish men were murdered because of this decree. Except for the few who were needed for forced labor, all of Serbia's Jewish men were killed.

Toward the end of 1941, over 8,000 Jewish women, CHILDREN, and elderly were still alive, mostly in the ghetto of Belgrade. They were sent to the camp at Semlin (Sajmiste) and gassed in the nearby woods. Within just over one year, almost all of Serbia's Jews had been murdered.

In August 1942, the German occupation authorities reported that the question of Serbian Jews had been "solved." The only Serbian Jews who remained alive were those who had hidden, or who had joined the partisans.

SEYSS-INQUART, ARTHUR

(1892–1946) Austrian Nazi. From 1918 he supported an Austro-German union and this led him to support the Nazis.

In 1936, he became an Austrian State councillor and worked to weaken the Austrian government. Even so, he won the trust of Austrian Chancellor Kurt von Schuschnigg. In February 1938, Seyss-Inquart became minister of the interior and of public security. On 11 March 1938, as Adolf HITLER was about to take over AUSTRIA, he notified Schuschnigg that he was being replaced by Seyss-Inquart. Hitler gave him the title of Reich Commissioner of Austria. However, he did not hold that position for long. In 1939–1940 he served in POLAND, as deputy governor.

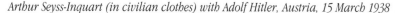

Arthur Seyss-Inquart (in civilian clothes) with Adolf Hitler, Austria, 15 March 1938

He then became Commissioner of the NETHERLANDS (1940–1945), where his energetic attempts to implement Hitler's policies, including those against the JEWS, alienated the population of the country. This did not stop him from stepping up anti-Jewish measures, from confiscation of properties to arrest and DEPORTATION to the Polish DEATH CAMPS. When it became clear that Germany was going to lose the war, Seyss-Inquart tried, without success, to enter negotiations with the Allied Powers. Tried at Nuremberg (see TRIALS OF WAR CRIMINALS) for war crimes, he was sentenced to death and executed in 1946.

S H A N G H A I

Port town in China, occupied by the Japanese from 1937. Shanghai became a refuge and transit point for thousands of Jewish REFUGEES from Nazi Europe, since it was one of the few places in the world that allowed entry without visas or landing permits.

Following the KRISTALLNACHT pogrom of November 1938, large numbers of refugees began arriving by sea. They remained in Shanghai or moved on to other destinations. After the Mediterranean was closed to civilian shipping in May 1940, several thousand refugees fled to Shanghai over land, via Siberia and Manchuria. Additional refugees were deported from Japan to Shanghai, following the Japanese declaration of war on the United States in December 1941. Afterward, immigration stopped and the refugee population in Shanghai remained stable at 17,000 until the war's end.

On 18 February 1943, under Nazi pressure, the Japanese moved Jewish refugees into a GHETTO. There they remained until the end of the war. Most of the refugee community were dependent on aid sent by Jewish relief agencies such as the AMERICAN JEWISH JOINT DISTRIBUTION COMMITTEE.

Despite economic hardship, the refugee community created a vibrant social, religious, and cultural life. It included the rabbis and teachers of one of the most famous talmudic academies in Lithuania—the Mir Yeshiva.

After the war, most refugees left for PALESTINE, the United States, and other destinations in countries of the western world.

Jews working at a grocery store in Shanghai, 1943

S H O A H

Hebrew term for the HOLOCAUST—the total destruction of the Jewish people and Jewish society in Europe by the Nazis during WORLD WAR II. The term *Shoah* means devastation and catastrophe. Many use it instead of the words Holocaust and *Hurban*, ("destruction," favored in certain religious circles), since these have religious and sacrificial meanings in traditional Jewish texts. The term *Shoah* began to be recognized widely after it was used as the title of Claude Lanzmann's major film on the subject. It first appeared in the booklet, *Shoat Yehudei Polin* ("The Devastation of Polish Jewry"), published in Jerusalem in 1940.

S I L E S I A

Region of POLAND that was annexed by GERMANY during WORLD WAR II.

Large Jewish communities, such as Bedzin and Sosnowiec, existed in Silesia. The JEWS of this region were targets of discrimination. They were ordered to wear a Jewish BADGE, men were drafted for FORCED LABOR, and property was confiscated.

While conditions were harsh, they were not as severe during the first years of the war as in other parts of Poland. Closed GHETTOS, for example, were not set up until the spring of 1943. Food rations were larger than in occupied Poland, and death rates were lower. This seemed to be due to the fact that Silesia was not considered part of Poland by the Germans. Some say it was because of the close relationship and cooperation between Silesia's JUDENRAT (Jewish Council) chairman, Moshe MERIN, and the Germans.

In January 1940, the Germans set up Silesia's Judenrat. The systematic murder of the Jews by DEPORTATION TO DEATH CAMPS, did not reach Silesia until May 1942. Merin obeyed German demands to have Jews report for deportation. He believed that by sacrificing part of the community he would save the majority of the Jews. The number sacrificed was quite large. By August 1942, one-third of the 100,000 Jews in Silesia had been sent to AUSCHWITZ (itself located in Silesia). Many of the smaller communities in the

Wehrmacht soldier detaining a Jew in Bytom, Silesia

region were liquidated. Those deported from the larger cities were mostly the sick, elderly, and impoverished. Of the Jews who were spared, many worked in German armaments factories or in workshops for the German war effort. Others were sent to forced LABOR CAMPS. Merin believed that by keeping Jews productive—and necessary to the Nazis— he could save their lives.

Jewish YOUTH MOVEMENTS, although prohibited, were very active in the region. The majority were Zionist. They ran agricultural training centers in the hope of one day becoming farmers in the Land of Israel.

Youth groups were among the most vocal in opposing Merin's policy of cooperation with the Germans. They also called for armed RESISTANCE, which the Judenrat opposed. In spring 1943, youth movement members were able to smuggle arms from WARSAW into the region. Weapons' training sessions were held. During that time, Merin handed over ten youth group members to the GESTAPO; all were executed. Although many ghetto residents were useful as laborers for the German war effort, the Nazis decided that the entire Jewish population of Silesia was to be destroyed.

In June 1943, Merin was deported to Auschwitz. The remaining Jews were deported throughout the summer. On 1 August, the Germans began to liquidate the Bedzin and Sosnowiec ghettos—the largest in the region.

In a little more than two weeks, over 30,000 Jews were deported to Auschwitz. This was carried out, however, with some Jewish resistance. Jews opened fire on the Germans at three separate times. In one instance, an SS man was killed by members of a Zionist youth movement. Many Jews went into hiding, but almost all were caught.

On 26 August, the Germans liquidated Zawiercie, the last Jewish community in Silesia, by deporting 2,500 Jews to Auschwitz.

At the end of 1943, about 100 members of youth movements, who had successfully hidden from the Germans, were able to escape from Silesia. They crossed the border into SLOVAKIA, and from there into HUNGARY. This last remnant of Silesian Jewry was then able to warn Jewish youth movements in Hungary of the fate that awaited them at the hands of the Nazis.

SIMON WIESENTHAL CENTER

An organization dedicated to preserving the meaning of the HOLOCAUST and to the defense of human rights and the Jewish people. Founded in 1977, it is headquartered in Los Angeles, with offices in New York, Toronto, Miami, Jerusalem and Paris.

The Center has developed programs in Holocaust education and research for schools, service organizations, media and international forums. It was involved in a key role in tracking down Nazis and Nazi collaborators who had escaped detection. In February 1993, the Center opened a technologically advanced museum, Beit Hashoah Museum of Tolerance, in Los Angeles. Innovative programming and interactive displays enable visitors to explore their own biases, learn about prejudice and racism in America, and study about antisemitism during WORLD WAR II as they confront the Holocaust in history. The Center serves as an important reminder that to neglect or forget the Nazi murder of JEWS and other minorities is done at our own peril. Threats to human rights, intolerance and genocide remain a serious challenge to us all.

SLOVAK NATIONAL UPRISING

A revolt that erupted in SLOVAKIA in August 1944. It was led by army officers, PARTISANS, and groups of escaped prisoners from various countries. They formed the National Slovak Council (SNR). The SNR called for an independent state of Slovakia, rather than the government of Jozef TISO, which collaborated with the Nazi rulers. Jewish fighting units in the Slovak LABOR CAMPS of NOVÁKY, Sered, and Vhyne made contact with the SNR early in 1944. They hoped that they could save the 20,000 JEWS still in the country.

Some 2,000 Jews fought in the uprising, and 500 of them died. Jews were among the leaders of the uprising and several served as unit commanders. Support from PALESTINE came in the form of four PARACHUTISTS sent from the Middle East to Slovakia. Three of them were killed in the uprising. The 60,000 Slovak rebels fought fiercely but were outnumbered by the strongly armed German troops. In October 1944, the revolt was finally put down by the Germans. As part of their "punishment," the

Germans rounded up Jews, killing many and sending others to DEATH CAMPS.

S L O V A K I A

The eastern region of CZECHOSLOVAKIA, which was a part of HUNGARY until 1918. The Germans took over the independent state of Czechoslovakia in 1939. Slovakia then became a satellite of Nazi GERMANY until April 1945.

In 1930, almost 137,000 JEWS lived in Slovakia. Many of them practiced traditional Orthodox Judaism and lived in the eastern part of the region. Slovak ANTISEMITISM was directed mostly at these Jews. Slovak nationalists considered the Jews of this region to be representatives of Hungarian culture. They also believed that the Jews were trying to get rich by exploiting them. In 1938, the Slovaks carried out violent night raids on their Jewish neighbors. They forced the Jews across the border into Hungary. The Hungarians, however, wanted nothing to do with the Jews and forced them back. This left them for weeks in the no-man's land between the two countries, until an arrangement could be made between the two countries.

When Germany occupied BOHEMIA AND MORAVIA, Slovakia was declared self-ruling. It was controlled by a totalitarian government known as the Slovak People's Party. The pro-Nazi priest Jozef TISO led this party. He called for Christian solidarity, extreme nationalism, and a social order supposedly based on Catholicism. Jews were attacked on the streets by the HLINKA GUARD, their homes and businesses looted, and synagogues destroyed.

Slovak Jews did their best to aid the REFUGEES in their country. Their Zionist leaders established the Central Jewish Bureau, which was officially recognized by the Slovak government. One of its main projects was to aid the Jews in the no-man's land. They also tried to help Jews escape from Slovakia, provided food, helped with housing, and became involved in education. However, many of these attempts to give aid ended when war broke out in September 1939.

In July 1940, Adolf HITLER demanded an increase in anti-Jewish activities. The Slovak government decided to become a National Socialist (Nazi) regime. This led to the introduction of ANTI-JEWISH LEGISLATION. However, in an attempt to appear independent of the Nazis, Tiso explained this legislation as a means

Preparing a Jewish transport from Zilina, Slovakia, to a concentration camp

of preserving the welfare of the Slovak people. At the same time, German advisors on matters of police, propaganda, and the Jews were added to the Slovak government. The oppression of Jews quickly followed. Many Jewish men were drafted into labor units of the Slovak army. The Central Economic Office was established to eliminate Jews from economic life and to "Aryanize" Jewish property (see ARYANIZATION). In late September 1940, the Center of Jews (Ústerdná Zidov, UZ) was founded as a government tool to organize Jewish life. The 175 Jewish organizations in Slovakia were closed down by the government and their funds were given to the UZ. The authorities sealed the Zionist Organization's doors. However, its members managed to smuggle out the lists of members and foreign correspondence which allowed them to continue their efforts underground.

After much debate, the Zionists joined the Orthodox Jews as members of the Center of Jews. Among their many difficult tasks, the UZ was ordered to establish LABOR CAMPS. The Jews were expected both to finance and build them. The department of occupational retraining used the camps as a cover for the Zionist YOUTH MOVEMENTS and their agricultural training programs. Despite Slovak government interference, the UZ managed to publish a newspaper, coordinate various Jewish youth activities, and maintain 70 branches scattered around the country.

When the Slovak army entered the war in the summer of 1941, anti-Jewish legislation grew worse. Jews were forced to wear the yellow BADGE. They were banned from many public places and a curfew was imposed. Many Jews were sent to labor camps. Slovakia was the first country to organize mass DEPORTATIONS. It is estimated that 58,700 Jews were sent to AUSCHWITZ in 1942 alone.

In February 1942, Hans Ludin, the German ambassador to Slovakia, requested a selection of 20,000 young Jews to "build new Jewish settlements." The Slovak government agreed, but it feared it would be left with only "unproductive" Jews. Therefore, it demanded that the entire Jewish population be deported. In return, the Nazis insisted that the equivalent of $1.8 million be paid by the Slovaks to cover the cost of "vocational training." At the same time, it promised that these Jews would never return and that no claims would be made to their property. Most of these Slovak Jews were sent to Auschwitz and MAJDANEK, and their property was seized.

Those who had escaped from Polish CONCENTRATION CAMPS brought reports to Jewish leaders about the fate of those deported. The leaders tried to halt the process by intervening with the government and the Roman Catholic Church. A secret unit of the was Jewish Council formed, calling itself the WORKING GROUP. Among the most important people in this UNDERGROUND organization were Gisi FLEISCHMANN and Rabbi Michael Dov WEISSMANDEL. They developed a plan of large-scale bribery. $50,000 was exchanged with Slovak officials in order to halt the deportations. This lasted from 1942 to 1944.

The Working Group came to realize that in order for the Jews to save themselves, they must become indispensable to the Germans and the Slovaks. Thus, factories and workshops were established in the NOVÁKY, Sered and Vyhne labor camps. In 1943, these camps had a total of 140 workshops. They made furniture, clothing, chemicals, toys, leather, and a variety of other products. They were managed by local Jewish councils. The councils also encouraged training to employ as many Jews as possible. The camps were guarded by Slovaks, but despite overcrowding, activities were conducted freely.

The men of the Slovak Sixth Army Brigade and some in the labor camps of Nováky, Sered and Vyhne began to arm themselves. Underground cells were formed in the labor camps. From August until October 1944, these units took part in the SLOVAK NATIONAL UPRISING aimed at freeing Slovakia from dependence on Nazi Germany. This uprising was, however, defeated and even harsher Nazi policies were put in place.

Embarrassed by the growth of anti-government activity, the Slovak government was quick to blame the Czechs, the Russians, and especially the Jews for the uprising. A manhunt for Jews began and deportation by rail was organized. Sered was declared a concentration camp and those who were rounded up were sent there and treated with particular cruelty. Yet, despite the brutality of the SS at Sered, the Working Group succeeded in continuing production at the camp. They were thus able to supply secretly those being deported with clothing and other necessities as well as providing other aid. Toward the end of 1944, women and children were transferred to THERESIENSTADT. By the end of March 1945, Sered was destroyed.

One hundred thousand Slovak Jews were killed under Nazi rule in Slovakia. When the survivors returned to their homes after the war and requested the return of their property, they were met with hostility and violence. The majority of Slovak survivors moved to ISRAEL in 1949.

S O B I B Ó R

DEATH CAMP designed and built for the sole purpose of killing JEWS. It was located in the LUBLIN district of POLAND, near the railway station of the village of Sobibór. It was built in a wooded, swampy area beginning in 1942.

SS commander Franz STANGL was appointed camp commandant in the spring of 1942. He had worked with murder before, in the so-called "EUTHANASIA PROGRAM" that killed—at times by gassing—mentally retarded and emotionally disturbed Germans. He was assisted by a staff of 20 to 30 Germans. Most of these were also experienced killers from the Euthanasia Program. They had additional help from 90 to 120 Ukrainians.

Entrance to the Sobibór Death Camp

The barbed wire fence of the camp was camouflaged by trees to hide the killing program. As in the other AKTION REINHARD camps, the killing process was

Model of the Sobibór death camp, made by Sasha Pechersky, leader of the Sobibór revolt, for a school in Soviet Russia

direct and systematic. Jews deported from GHETTOS by train would arrive in the station. From there they were marched to the reception area, known as camp II. There they would undress, their possessions were confiscated, and women's hair was cut. The prisoners were then sent naked down a 492-foot path to the GAS CHAMBERS, where they were murdered. Gold was extracted from teeth and the property left behind was sorted and packed for shipment. The bodies were buried in large trenches.

Between May and the end of July 1942, 90,000 to 100,000 Jews from Lublin in Poland and from CZECHOSLOVAKIA, GERMANY, and AUSTRIA were killed at Sobibór. Killing was halted temporarily so the gas chambers could be enlarged to hold 1,200 persons at a time. Then the killing began again. The Jewish victims of the expanded killing operations were mostly from eastern Galicia, SLOVAKIA, the NETHERLANDS, and the VILNA, MINSK, and Lida Ghettos. At the end of the summer of 1942, the bodies of dead Jews were dug up and burned (see AKTION 1005).

On 5 July 1943, Heinrich HIMMLER personally ordered the closing of Sobibór, since its task was complete. Shortly before the camp was closed, an uprising of inmates took place. Lieutenant Sasha Pechersky, a former Soviet army officer, who had arrived at Sobibór, together with Leon Feldhendler, leader of the Sobibór RESISTANCE, carried out a plan. The SS officers would be killed, their weapons seized and the Jews would fight their way out of the camp. The uprising took place on 14 October 1943. Eleven SS men and several Ukrainians were killed. More than 300 Jews escaped. Most were caught by German troops or turned in by Polish civilians. Many perished in the cold. Only 50 Sobibór prisoners survived the war.

By the end of 1943, no trace of Sobibór was left. The camp area was plowed under and a farm put in its place. The area was liberated by the Soviet army in summer 1944.

Eleven of the SS men who had served in Sobibór were tried in West Germany, between September 1965 and December 1966. One committed suicide; one was sentenced to life imprisonment; five were given sentences ranging from three to eight years' imprisonment; and four were acquitted. The area of the camp was declared a national shrine by the Polish government and a memorial was erected there.

SONDERKOMMANDO

("Special Commando")

Term that was used for a detachment of the SS or EINSATZGRUPPEN. It is best known, however, as the name for the groups of Jews in DEATH CAMPS who had to remove bodies from the GAS CHAMBERS for burial or cremation.

Jewish Sonderkommando existed in nearly all the Nazi death camps, sometimes under other names, such as corpse commando or body commando. Their job was to carry out much of the manual work connected with the process of mass murder and looting the bodies.

Sonderkommando aided in "preparing" Jews before their entry into the gas chambers. Sonderkommando barbers cut the hair of the women (before or after death). Others collected and sorted the victims' personal possessions and prepared them for shipment to GERMANY. The Sonderkommando removed the bodies from the gas chambers, extracted gold dental fillings, and carried the corpses to the crematoria or pits. They also cleaned the gas chambers to destroy evidence of the killing that took place in them.

The Sonderkommando themselves were periodically killed and replaced by new arrivals. In death camps such as BELZEC, about 2 to 3 percent of new arrivals were assigned to the Sonderkommando. All the rest were killed immediately. In order to enable them to carry out their work, Sonderkommando usually received better food than the other prisoners. They were also allowed to keep some of the food they found among the belongings of those being killed.

Sonderkommando participated in the TREBLINKA revolt in June 1943. In October 1944, a team of the AUSCHWITZ-Birkenau Sonderkommando carried out a revolt that resulted in the destruction of one of the crematoria and the death of several German guards. Some prisoners also escaped during the revolt, but all were hunted down and killed.

Although some Jews resented the Sonderkommando for their "cooperation" in the killing process, the fact is that they never had any choice in the matter. Almost all Sonderkommando were themselves destined to be put to death at some stage. Today, there are only several dozen survivors of this gruesome work.

Jews from France in a Sonderkommando in the Belzec Death Camp

SOUSA MENDES, ARISTIDES DE

(1885–1954) Portuguese diplomat working in Bordeaux, FRANCE,who saved Jews during WORLD WAR II.

When northern France fell to the Germans in May 1940, a wave of Jewish and non-Jewish REFUGEES flooded southern France. Many of them tried to escape Nazi persecution there by fleeing Europe through Portuguese ports. To reach ports such as Lisbon, however, they had to travel through SPAIN. A Portuguese transit or entry visa was needed to pass the Spanish border. In May 1940, the Portuguese government ordered its diplomats in France to stop granting visas to refugees seeking shelter from the Nazis, especially JEWS.

As the German army advanced toward Bordeaux, Sousa Mendes disobeyed his government's order. He used his office as consul general to issue almost 10,000 visas to Jewish and non-Jewish refugees seeking to flee France. Furious at his act of defiance, the government of PORTUGAL dismissed him from his diplomatic post and ordered him to return to Lisbon.

Sousa Mendes held no regrets. "I am a Catholic," he said, "and as a Catholic I cannot act otherwise." He was stripped of his government pension, and left to care for his family of 13 children. He died a poor man.

YAD VASHEM honored him in 1966 as a "RIGHTEOUS AMONG THE NATIONS." In 1988, the Portuguese National Assembly voted to restore his good reputation.

SOVIET JEWISH ANTI-FASCIST COMMITTEE

Jewish organization in SOVIET RUSSIA from 1942 to 1948. The committee's official purpose was to gather support from world Jewry for the Soviet war effort, although its activities eventually included domestic as well as international goals.

Before 1941, the communists in Russia had opposed any Jewish body that spoke for the JEWS or represented a form of Jewish organization. However, after Russia was attacked by GERMANY in June 1941, Russia worked actively for the support of the western Allies. This included appealing to Jews in the west. So, in spring 1942, the Jewish Anti-Fascist Committee was formed with the support of the Soviet authorities. The committee's formation symbolized acceptance of Soviet Jewry by the Soviet government, and was welcomed by the Jews as a sign of Jewish national solidarity. The noted Yiddish actor Solomon Mikhoels was appointed chairman after a conference that was attended by delegates representing the Jewish population of Soviet Russia. One of its most prominent leaders was Itzik Feffer, a Red Army colonel and poet. Mikhoels and Feffer were sent to GREAT BRITAIN, Mexico, CANADA, and the United States with Joseph STALIN's blessing in 1943, to plead for active Jewish support for the Russian war effort. They were welcomed by Jewish organizations. They were given opportunities to address large Jewish gatherings and to collect several million dollars' worth of aid for the Red Army and Soviet civilians. Arriving in New York, the two Soviet Jewish leaders spoke at a ceremony before 50,000 persons. The committee was also active inside the Soviet Union. It raised Jewish issues with the authorities, documented the HOLOCAUST and, in the later stages of the war, worked to restore Jewish life.

After the war, Soviet Russia entered a cold war with the West, at which point the committee's usefulness ended. It came to be viewed as a threat by the Soviet authorities because of its Jewish identity. Stalin adopted a vigorous anti-Jewish policy and the leaders of the committee were among his prime targets. Mikhoels was murdered by the secret police in January 1948, although the murder was presented as an accident. The Anti-Fascist Committee was dis-

solved in November 1948. Its members were imprisoned and executed along with the country's outstanding Jewish poets and writers in 1952.

SOVIET PRISONERS OF WAR

From the time of the German attack on SOVIET RUSSIA in June 1941 until the end of the war in 1945, the German army took approximately 5.7 million Soviet prisoners of war. Of these, 3.3 million died. By the end of the first winter alone, 2 million had died. Those who survived were shipped back to GERMANY to work as forced laborers under terrible conditions. The treatment of Soviet prisoners of war was one of the worst Nazi crimes. It was a product of the especially savage campaign of the Germans against the Soviets (see Operation BARBAROSSA).

From the start, the Nazis were prepared to allow millions of Soviet prisoners and citizens to die. As a result, they made no preparations for the large numbers of prisoners that they took in the first months. Prisoners were sent, under dreadful conditions, to camps without proper shelter, clothing or food. They died of hunger, illness and exposure. In

Soviet prisoners of war in a camp near Kharkov

their initial joy over their victories in the east, the Nazis saw no need to keep Soviets alive for use as laborers.

By late 1941, however, there was a serious labor shortage in German industry. The Nazis were forced to ship Soviet prisoners back to Germany to use as FORCED LABOR. From early 1942, hundreds of thousands of Soviet prisoners of war and civilians were sent from German-occupied areas of Soviet Russia to Germany to work in armaments factories. Although the Germans now wanted to keep the prisoners alive, conditions remained dreadful. Prisoners were forced to carry out long hours of hard physical work for next to no pay. German businesses were more than willing to use these helpless victims.

SOVIET RUSSIA

Country (also known as the Soviet Union) extending from eastern Europe across the whole length of Asia. In 1917, as a result of revolution, Russia fell under communist rule. This regime sought to deprive the JEWS of their heritage. Jewish religious practice and teaching were forbidden, as was the study of Hebrew. The Jews were no longer allowed to have their own community and the three million Jews of Russia were cut off from Jews in the rest of the world. After Adolf HITLER came to power in 1933, communist Russia and Nazi GERMANY were deadly enemies. However, in August 1939, to everyone's amazement, they signed the NAZI-SOVIET PACT. This enabled Hitler to attack POLAND without fear of Russian intervention. In return, Russia received considerable territories, including the Baltic countries of LITHUANIA, LATVIA, and ESTONIA which had a large Jewish populations. The Jews in these countries suffered from Soviet Russia's economic policies, but at least they were spared the horrors of persecution and mass murder suffered by Jews under the Germans. However, this proved to be only a temporary situation. On 22 June 1941, Hitler launched a surprise attack (Operation BARBAROSSA) on Soviet Russia and soon overran all the areas that had been annexed by Russia, as well as most of the European parts of Russia. They reached the gates of Moscow and Leningrad before the winter of 1941.

The Germans claimed that their attack was de-

Russian partisan unit in Kiev

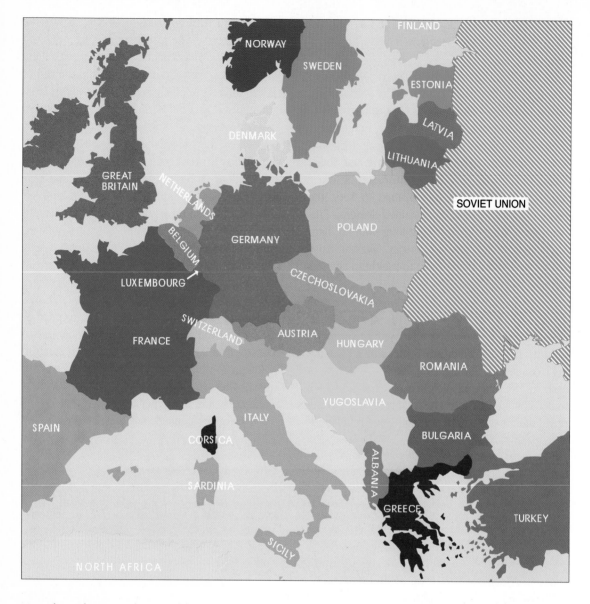

signed to eliminate their "Bolshevik and Jewish" enemy, to conquer "living space" (LEBENSRAUM) for themselves in the East, and to establish "New Order" in Europe based on Nazi racial doctrines and terror. The assault marked a new stage in the HOLOCAUST—the implementation of the "FINAL SOLUTION," the total extermination of the Jews. Mass executions, in the form of open-air shooting, was the dominant pattern in German-occupied Soviet Russia. In Poland, DEATH CAMPS equipped with GAS CHAMBERS functioned as the main form of organized mass murder. Many Jews from Russia died there.

Special German task forces were called in, commissioned with the task of liquidating Jews, communists, and other "enemies" of the German Reich, such as GYPSIES and the mentally ill. Following the advancing German army, the mobile killing units consisted of the SS EINSATZGRUPPEN of the Security Police and Security Service, the brigades of the Waffen-SS (see glossary), and the police battalions of the German Police. In fulfilling their mission, they could rely on close cooperation with German military and civilian authorities, as well as on the indispensable services offered by local COLLABORATORS. Jew-haters were encouraged to instigate POGROMS. A wave of violent acts erupted, affecting many communities both in cities and rural areas.

The spontaneous outburst of Jew-hatred was followed by a planned and systematic process of persecution and extermination. In the initial phase of Operation Barbarossa, adult Jewish men were shot, accused of being "snipers," "looters," "agitators," or "traitors." Such terms were deliberately used in an attempt to justify murders as "punitive measures" or "cleansing operations." Very quickly, the perpetrators became accustomed to systematic killing. In August 1941, women fell victim to killing actions. Soon afterward, as a final logical step, CHILDREN were targeted for murdering. Just as quickly, efforts were made to clear the whole region of Jews. By late 1941, reports were proudly submitted that large areas had already been made "*Judenfrei*" (free of Jews). Due to the lack of manpower and the restrictions of mass executions, not all Jews could be killed in one gigantic sweep. The specific conditions prevailing in the conquered territories, such as harsh winter conditions, the remoteness of Jewish settlements in rural areas, and the need for Jewish labor, required more time. The Jews spared from the first wave of killing were marked with yellow BADGES and imprisoned in GHETTOS or CAMPS, exposed to ill-treatment, starvation, and FORCED LABOR.

In spring 1942, mass executions began again. A second killing wave swept through the occupied Soviet Russia. By the end of 1943, the process of the liquidation of ghettos and camps had almost been completed. Everywhere search commandos hunted down Jews who had escaped into the underground and forests where they attempted to join the Soviet PARTISANS or to establish Jewish FAMILY CAMPS. Efforts were made by units of a special SS commando group (AKTION 1005) to eradicate all evidence pointing to mass murder by digging up the mass graves and burning the human remains. Numerous SS and police men, together with officials from the other German agencies, implemented the program of the "Final Solution." They were further assisted by local collaborators and Jew-haters.

An organized Jewish resistance movement in Russia proved impossible. In the previous decades, all Jewish organizations had been banned and so the Jews lacked any structure which could plan group resistance. Moreover, most Jewish men were fighting in the Russian army (the Red Army), where they had a glorious record of heroism, some rising to very high positions and more than 160,000 winning

decorations. Individual Jews fled to the forests and joined the Russian partisans. Sometimes entire families escaped and established family camps.

Many Jews succeeded in fleeing to the interior of Russia, often in Asia. These included a large number who had fled eastward from Poland and the Baltic States before the German invasion of Russia. From the end of 1942, the tide of war turned and the Germans were pushed back without reaching these parts or even breaking into Moscow or Leningrad. During the war, the Russian dictator, Joseph STALIN, established the Soviet JEWISH ANTI-FASCIST COMMITTEE— the first Jewish body recognized by the authorities for a long time—and this served as a focus for bringing Jews together. Under the impending danger of the Holocaust, Jews in unoccupied Russia developed Jewish nationalistic feelings, which had previously been banned. This was to prove crucial for the future of Soviet Jewry. They realized that Soviet Russia's prewar boast that it had destroyed ANTI-SEMITISM was meaningless. This was especially disproved by the expressions of antisemitism and the extent of collaboration with the Nazis among the Russian population during the war. Jewish identity became strengthened. This in turn was to lead, after the war, to a strong persecution of Jews by Stalin. This only strengthened the Jews' national identification and was eventually to lead to the mass exodus of a high proportion once they were allowed to leave.

About one million Soviet Jews were killed in the Holocaust.

SOVIET UNION

see SOVIET RUSSIA.

SPAIN

Country in western Europe. From 1936 to 1939, Spain had suffered a civil war in which right-wing forces led by General Francisco Franco, aided by Nazi GERMANY and Fascist ITALY, had succeeded in defeating the army of the democratically elected government supported by SOVIET RUSSIA. On 1 April 1939, General Franco declared the end of the civil war and became the head of the Spanish state. Spain was devastated by the war. People were starving and many areas were destroyed. Hundreds of thou-

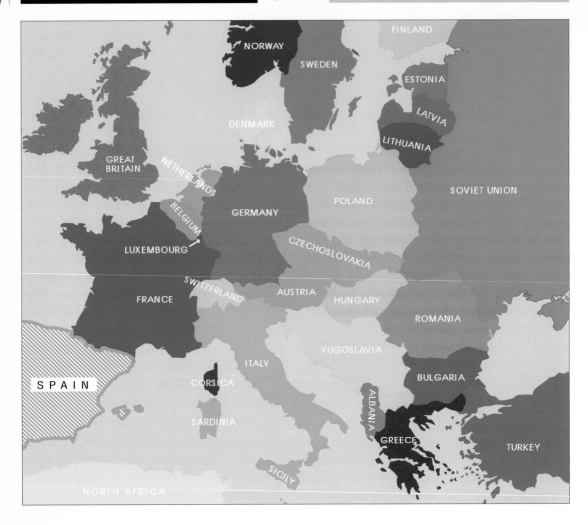

sands had died and tens of thousands were in prison. Many of these were about to be executed by the new nationalistic government, which was allied with Germany and Italy. Some 6,000 JEWS had lived in Spain before July 1936, when the civil war began. Many of them had been REFUGEES from Germany but very few remained. Like all other non-Catholics, they did not have the right to worship as Jews or maintain any organization.

In June 1940, when FRANCE was defeated, hundreds of thousands of refugees fled the advancing Nazi army. Spain became the main route to rescue. Refugees who had a Portuguese visa or had reservations to sail from Spanish ports were allowed to cross through Spain. There was no official discrimination against Jewish refugees, although Spanish officials did sometimes make it difficult for them. It is estimated that the number of Jews who crossed through Spain from June 1940 to summer 1942,

reached several tens of thousands. No Jewish organization was allowed to work in Spain on behalf of the refugees.

When DEPORTATIONS TO DEATH CAMPS began in France in the summer of 1942, Jewish refugees from France began to stream across the Pyrenee mountains. The Spanish authorities soon discovered that they were Jewish and planned to force them back to France. However, the Allies became concerned with their fate. Spain gave in to pressure from the United States and GREAT BRITAIN. All of the refugees were allowed to stay, although they were be held in prison. The Allies supported them and guaranteed that they would be moved later to other places. A special agency working under the American Embassy was allowed to act on the behalf of the Jewish refugees. It was financed mainly by the AMERICAN JEW-ISH JOINT DISTRIBUTION COMMITTEE. It is estimated that some 7,500 Jews from all nations were saved by

Jewish children rescued from France in Barcelona, Spain

crossing into Spain from July 1942 to September 1944.

Some 4,000 Jews who possessed Spanish documents lived in various European countries occupied by Germany. They were technically Spanish nationals and therefore could be saved by Spain. Almost all of them were Sephardi Jews who had preserved the Spanish language and heritage through four and a half centuries. However, when Germany offered Spain the opportunity to bring them "home" to Spain, it became obvious that Spain did not really want them. Only some 800 of these Jews were brought there under the condition that they would not remain permanently.

When the mass murder of Hungarian Jewry reached its peak, in the summer and fall of 1944, Spanish representatives in BUDAPEST, along with other neutral countries, issued thousands of documents to Jews which saved their lives.

SPEER, ALBERT

(1905–1981) Architect and Nazi Minister of Armaments from 1942 to 1945. Speer joined the Nazi Party in 1931. An ambitious architect, he was awarded contracts to renovate the Nazi Party headquarters in Berlin and the Propaganda Ministry building. He later built the setting for all the Nazi Party rallies in Nuremberg. The oversized grandeur of these structures, which he called "cathedrals of

Hitler with Professor Gall and Albert Speer (right) inspect the progress on the House of German Art in Munich

light," was in keeping with Nazi style. Adolf HITLER planned to develop Berlin into a city of monuments and turned to Speer directly. It was a perfect match, since Hitler saw in Speer "an architect of genius" and said that "for the opportunity to do a great building, he would sell his soul to the devil like Faust." Speer built the Chancellery which was destroyed in the bombardment of Berlin at the end of the war.

In 1937, Speer was appointed inspector general of construction of the Reich's capital. In 1942, he became Minister of Armaments and War Production. Both posts allowed him to use slave labor and materials stolen from Europe's Jewish population. Speer was a personal favorite of Hitler, so much so that Hitler made him second in succession after Hermann GÖRING.

At the conclusion of the war, Speer was arrested and tried in the TRIALS OF WAR CRIMINALS at Nuremberg for war crimes and for using forced laborers and CONCENTRATION CAMP prisoners in his work. Unlike most other Nuremberg defendants, although he refused to admit that he knew about the mass killings in eastern Europe, Speer expressed regret about his crimes. He said, "I don't believe there can be any atonement in this lifetime for sins of such huge dimension." He was convicted on both counts and

served a 20-year sentence in Spandau prison. By contrast, Fritz SAUCKEL, Speer's assistant, was tried on similar counts and executed.

In 1970, following his release from prison, Speer published *Inside the Third Reich*, his personal memoirs. In it, he restates his sense of repentance.

SS ("Schutzstaffel")

("Protection Squad")

The organization within the Nazi Reich responsible for carrying out all aspects of the "FINAL SOLUTION" and other acts of terror.

The SS was originally formed in 1923 as the personal bodyguard of Adolf HITLER. For most of that decade, it was the lesser of the two Nazi militias, second to the SA brown-shirts. However, in 1929, Heinrich HIMMLER became its national leader. Under his leadership, the SS became dominant. Its members wore black shirts and the DEATH'S HEAD insignia. Himmler opened many new departments, including the organization's intelligence service (the SD), took over the GESTAPO and the SA, and made the CONCENTRATION CAMP system flourish. During the war, the organization grew tremendously.

SS men were the elite of the Nazi empire. There

SS unit marching in Warsaw

were two important requirements for membership. The first was unconditional loyalty to Hitler. The second was complete "racial purity" (see RACISM). SS officers had to prove their racial purity and that of their wives—dating back to the year 1700. They also had to be "appropriately Aryan" in their appearance. By 1939, the SS had hundreds of thousands of members.

The SS's Race and Resettlement Main Office was in charge of all matters of racial purity. It checked the lineage of SS members. It was also responsible for resettling the conquered areas of Europe with "Aryans." It directed centers for reproducing a pure race, and eventually also MEDICAL EXPERIMENTS and the EUTHANASIA PROGRAM. Finally, the murderous EINSATZ-GRUPPEN were formed from its ranks. Its REICHSSICHER-HEITSHAUPTAMT (RSHA; Reich Security Main Office) was responsible for internal security, killing enemies of the Nazis during the early period of conquests, and sending prisoners to concentration camps. Its chief expert on Jews was Adolf EICHMANN and it was responsible for sending Jews to the DEATH CAMPS. SS officers were involved in all aspects of the "Final Solution." This included the mobile killing units, which operated alongside regular troops, the concentration camps, and DEPORTATIONS. Eventually, the SS had millions of officials and soldiers under its command.

At the TRIALS OF WAR CRIMINALS at Nuremberg, the SS was treated as a criminal organization. This meant that its officers and members could be prosecuted. Some of its heads were sentenced to death, others to long periods of imprisonment, but many of these received amnesty.

STALIN, JOSEPH VISSARIONOVICH

(1879–1953) Ruler of SOVIET RUSSIA. Born in Georgia, Stalin joined the revolutionary movement in 1899 and was a leader of the communist Bolsheviks before World War I. After the Russian Revolution of October 1917, he became a member of the Politburo (the main committee of the Bolshevik Party). After a decade of political struggles and maneuvers, Stalin rose to be the undisputed national leader in 1928.

Stalin used "total terror" to enforce the extreme, revolutionary policies that he introduced in Soviet Russia. Anyone believed to oppose him was immediately imprisoned. His enemies were charged with crimes that were often invented by police and were

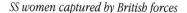

SS women captured by British forces

Above: Poster of Stalin overlooking a May Day parade in Moscow, 1945

Cartoon by David Low from World War II

given "show trials" designed to discourage other opponents. He ordered the murder of suspected enemies, including a whole generation of Jewish communists.

In the 1930s, Stalin was completely hostile to Nazism. However, in August 1939, he took the totally unexpected step of agreeing to the NAZI-SOVIET PACT. This agreement allowed Adolf HITLER to invade POLAND without opposition from Soviet Russia. It provided for the division of Poland between GERMANY and Soviet Russia. After the pact was signed, the Soviets also stopped criticizing Nazi persecution of the JEWS and increased their own anti-Jewish propaganda.

Stalin's naive trust of Hitler was betrayed when the Nazis invaded Soviet Russia in June 1941. Despite the massive defeats of 1941–1942, the Soviets recovered under the military and political leadership of Stalin, and the Germans were gradually beaten back. Stalin now needed the support of the Jews in the western world as well as in his own country. He therefore stopped his persecution of them and founded the SOVIET JEWISH ANTI-FASCIST COMMITTEE.

Stalin heavily influenced the new order of the world after the chaos of WORLD WAR II. He and the other Allied leaders shaped the future map of Europe at a series of conferences. In 1947, he tended to support the creation of the Jewish State of ISRAEL. He believed that it could be a Soviet satellite state. As it became clear that this would not happen, Stalin withdrew his support. Once again, his ANTISEMITISM became dominant. When the cold war began, he linked Jews with the United States (now his enemy) and became paranoid about Jews. All remaining Soviet Jewish organizations were shut down, leading Jews were arrested and executed, and many were exiled to Siberia. Stalin was planning a large-scale persecution of the Jews of Russia, but died before this could be carried out.

STANGL, FRANZ

(1908–1971) Nazi DEATH CAMP commander. Born in AUSTRIA, Stangl joined the Austrian police in 1931. He became a criminal investigator in the political division. His career as a Nazi murderer began in the so-called "EUTHANASIA PROGRAM," the systematic murder of

Franz Stangl

mentally retarded, handicapped, and incurably ill German citizens. As the program grew, 6 killing centers were established and at least 200,000 Germans were murdered.

Stangl was assigned to the first of the AKTION REINHARD death camps, BELZEC. He assumed command of SOBIBÓR in the spring of 1942. Later that year, he became commandant of TREBLINKA, where between 750,000 and 877,000 Jews were killed.

After the war, he was imprisoned by the Americans for belonging to the SS. In 1947, when the Austrians began investigating the Euthanasia Program, he was transferred to a civilian camp. From there he escaped to Syria and then Brazil. He lived and worked in Brazil for 16 years until his presence became known. He was arrested and brought to GERMANY in 1967. He was tried in 1969–1970, and sentenced to life in prison, where he died.

STATISTICS

The first statistical survey of European Jewry prepared by the Nazis was presented on 20 January 1942 at the WANNSEE CONFERENCE in BERLIN. Originally scheduled for the previous autumn, it had been

Estimated Jewish Losses in the Holocaust

COUNTRY	INITIAL JEWISH POPULATION	KILLED
Austria	185,000	50,000
Belgium	65,700	28,900
Bohemia and Moravia	118,310	78,150
Bulgaria	50,000	0
Denmark	7,800	60
Estonia	4,500	2,000
Finland	2,000	7
France	350,000	77,320
Germany	566,000	141,500
Greece	77,380	67,000
Hungary	825,000	569,000
Italy	44,500	7,680
Latvia	91,500	71,500
Lithuania	168,000	143,000
Luxembourg	3,500	1,950
Netherlands	140,000	100,000
Norway	1,700	762
Poland	3,300,000	3,000,000
Romania	609,000	287,000
Slovakia	88,950	71,000
Soviet Union	3,020,000	1,100,000
Yugoslavia	78,000	63,300
Total	9,796,840	5,860,129

postponed because of the failed advance on Moscow and the Japanese attack on Pearl Harbor. A month before, in KRAKÓW, Hans FRANK, the German Governor-General of POLAND, delivered a speech to his SS hierarchy. He said, "We have approximatly 2.5 million JEWS and now perhaps 3.5 million together with persons who have Jewish kin, and so on. We cannot shoot these 3.5 million Jews, we cannot poison them, but we will be able to take measures that will lead somehow to their destruction...when and how I will report to you when the time comes."

The historical accepted figure of six million Jews is composed of three elements: approximately 2.75–3.5m perishing in the extermination camps,

1.5–2m shot by the EINSATZGRUPPEN in POLAND, Russia, the Balkans and the Baltic, as well as 0.5–0.75m dying of hunger, disease and exposure in the ghettos of Eastern Europe. The difference between 4.75m and 6.25m was echoed by EICHMANN himself. In 1944 he told an ss colleague that six million were dead. In 1962, at his trial in ISRAEL, he said that the total was 5m. Precision is difficult, given the chaotic nature of HITLER's regime and its war effort.

Researchers into the HOLOCAUST have had many problems in determining the exact number of Jews who perished but all have ended up with a figure of between five and six million. It is particularly important to find accurate figures as a favorite claim of those who deny the Holocaust (see HOLOCAUST DENIAL) is to downplay the number killed (some say "only a million died, for example." The table is based on the "Encyclopedia of the Holocaust" which gathered figures from Holocaust researchers for each country.

S T E R I L I Z A T I O N

Surgical procedure that leaves a patient unable to reproduce. As early as 1933, the "Law for the Protection of German Heritage" gave the Nazi government the right to sterilize people with hereditary or genetic diseases. The Nazis wished to destroy as quickly as possible people who could be a threat to what they called the "racial health" of the German people. By 1937, 200,000 young men and women had been sterilized.

In 1942, experiments began in large-scale sterilization. These were directed at Jews and other groups earmarked by the Nazis for extermination. They were also a solution for the Nazis to the problem of the MISCHLINGE—people of partly Jewish ancestry, who could be used for FORCED LABOR. By sterilization, they would be allowed to live but it could be insured that their Jewish blood would not be transmitted to a new generation.

Heinrich HIMMLER asked the doctors at the CONCENTRATION CAMPS to develop methods of mass sterilization. Experiments in sterilization were carried out at AUSCHWITZ, Birkenau, and RAVENSBRÜCK. They involved bombarding the prisoners with x-rays, castration and chemical injections and were usually extremely painful.

The most infamous practitioner in the area of mass sterilization was Dr. Carl Clauberg at Auschwitz and Ravensbrück. He was tried by the Russians in 1948 and sentenced to 25 years in prison. Like most other Nazi doctors, his MEDICAL EXPERIMENTS were found to have little or no scientific value. Their clear purpose was to serve racist Nazi ideology, which made them obviously criminal.

S T R E I C H E R ,   J U L I U S

(1885–1946) Nazi leader. Streicher was the founder, editor and publisher of *Der* STÜRMER, an antisemitic, pornographic, scandalous Nazi newspaper.

Streicher was originally a school teacher who had become very involved in the Nazi Party as early as 1922. He had his students stand and shout "HEIL HITLER" when he entered the classroom each morning. He was removed from his position for "behavior unbecoming a teacher" in 1928. In January 1933, he was elected to the REICHSTAG, the German parliament, to represent the Nazi Party.

He launched his newspaper, *Der Stürmer*, in 1923. Almost every issue of the paper contained stories of how JEWS stole from Germans and contained cartoons of Jews shown as devils. It portrayed Jews as having kidnapped and raped young German Christians. The newspaper repeated the ancient libel that the Jews had killed JESUS and reprinted the medieval lies that Jews murdered Christian children and used their blood to bake unleavened bread for Passover.

Streicher was frequently in court defending himself against libel suits. This annoyed high-level Nazi leadership. In addition, other high ranking officials disliked Streicher's pornography and public scandals as well as his problematic business deals. In 1939, Adolf HITLER had to forbid him from making public statements. In 1940, Hermann GÖRING appointed a commission to investigate Streicher's life and dealings. The commission decided that his scandals were harmful to the Nazi Party and Streicher was removed from all party positions.

Streicher was tried at the NUREMBERG TRIAL. He was found not guilty of "conspiring to wage war," because he was not a military advisor to Hitler. However, he was found guilty of CRIMES AGAINST HUMANITY and was sentenced to death.

On 16 October 1946, as Streicher ascended to the gallows in Nuremberg for his execution, he shouted *"Purimfest"* and *"Heil Hitler."* *Purimfest* is German for the festival of Purim, which recalls the victory of the Persian Jews over their enemy, the tyrant Haman, in Bible times. Streicher was implying that the Jews would celebrate his execution.

STROOP, JÜRGEN

(1895–1951) ss and police leader who supervised the crushing of the WARSAW GHETTO UPRISING and the demolition of the GHETTO.

Stroop had been a brave and committed soldier in World War I. His nationalism was part of his reason for joining the Nazi Party and the SS in 1932. By 1939, he had risen to the rank of senior colonel. He enlisted to fight on the Russian front in 1941, but an injury restricted him to police duties in the occupied Soviet territory. Here he became known for his brutality in putting down PARTISAN activities, which included widespread persecution of the local population.

In April 1943, Stroop was transferred to WARSAW to take part in the liquidation of the ghetto. He became assistant to the SS and police leader, who was unable to cope with the desperate Jewish revolt. Stroop was put in charge. On 23 April, SS chief, Heinrich HIMMLER, ordered that "the Warsaw ghetto was to be searched with the greatest severity and brutal thoroughness." The Jewish rebellion lasted for 28 days.

However, the massive German military presence guaranteed that the rebellion would eventually be put down. Stroop commanded a fully armed force of 2,000 men and artillery. In the last of his daily progress reports, on 16 May, Stroop declared that the *aktion* ("operation") had been completed. The main synagogue had been blown up and 56,065 Jews captured or killed. More than 5,000 were sent to the TREBLINKA DEATH CAMP.

In September 1943, Stroop was transferred to GREECE to serve as SS and Police Leader. He was only there for a few weeks, but he helped with the DEPORTATIONS of Greek JEWS to AUSCHWITZ. He was arrested after the war and tried by an American Military Court and then the Warsaw District Court. He was sentenced to death and hanged.

Jürgen Stroop in captivity after the War

"STRUMA"

Boat used to help JEWS escape from German-occupied Europe. The *Struma* was an old cargo ship, which had sailed along the Danube river ferrying cattle. The organizers of ALIYA BET—the "illegal" immigrant movement run from PALESTINE—hired the *Struma* to bring Jewish HOLOCAUST REFUGEES from the Balkans to the shores of Palestine.

On 12 December 1941, the *Struma* left the port of Constanta, ROMANIA, on the Black Sea, overloaded with 769 passengers. No adequate preparation had been made for the long journey. The *Struma* had not been built to carry of human beings. It lacked the most basic facilities. Not only were there no toilets, but there was also no kitchen to cook food for such a large number of people. Officially, the *Struma* was bound for Istanbul in Turkey, since it did not have permission to bring Jews to Palestine. However, the passengers had no visas for Turkey either. After the massacres in BESSARABIA and BUKOVINA,

Romanian certificate of David Stoliar, the sole survivor of the "Struma"

Jews were desperate to get away at any cost and hoped that representatives of Jewish organizations in Istanbul would be able to obtain the necessary permits for them. The *Struma* developed engine trouble and barely reached Istanbul. The passengers were not allowed to land, since they did not have visas. Turkish authorities refused to let them settle in a temporary transit camp, even though it would be entirely funded by Jewish organizations. The refugees remained on board for ten weeks, subsisting on food and supplies provided by Jewish organizations. Negotiations carried on by representatives of these organizations with the Turkish and British authorities led nowhere. Public pressure also did not help the situation. The British were afraid to encourage a pattern of such sea escapes, and refused to grant visas to Palestine. For the same reason, the Turks would not let the refugees off the boat. On 23 February 1942, the Turkish authorities decided to get rid of the problem by sending the *Struma* on its way. The ancient boat was towed to the open sea, once again with no adequate prepara-tion, and left to fend for itself. It contained no food, no fuel, and not even water. On the same day, the *Struma* was hit by a torpedo and quickly sank. There was only one survivor. For many years, the identity of the submarine that fired the torpedo remained a mystery. Today, it is generally acknowledged that it was a Soviet submarine that mistook the refugee ship for a German boat.

"S T Ü R M E R,   D E R"

("The Stormer")

A Nazi newspaper that was founded, edited and published by Julius STREICHER in 1923. It was issued until the fall of Adolf HITLER and Nazi GERMANY.

Streicher was one of the most extreme anti-semites in the upper ranks of Hitler's henchmen. In *Der Stürmer* he spread hatred and his anti-Jewish, sadistic view of the world.

Der Stürmer was said to have been Hitler's favorite newspaper. Streicher claimed that it was the only paper that Hitler read from cover to cover.

"Der Stürmer" kiosk with the slogans "With the Stürmer against the Jews" and "The Jews are our misfortune"

The newspaper was illustrated with pornographic drawings. Its columns were filled with sex scandals and stories about the rapes of young Christian girls by JEWS. Almost every issue was full of exaggerated cartoons of Jews shown as swindlers, demons, money grubbers, and seducers of innocent German Christians. Among its standard lies was its claim to have found clear evidence that Jesus was not a Jew. In May 1937, *Der Stürmer* claimed that the crash of a German airship, the *Hindenburg*, in the United States was the result of a Jewish conspiracy to destroy all that was German.

S T U T T H O F

German CONCENTRATION CAMP in northern POLAND. It was established in 1939 in an isolated wooded area along the Baltic Sea.

At first, Stutthof was a civilian prison camp run by the German police chief from nearby DANZIG (Gdánsk). In January 1942, it officially became a concentration camp. The camp guards consisted of SS men (DEATH'S HEAD UNITS) and Ukrainian helpers.

Tens of thousands of men and women—perhaps as many as 100,000—were deported to the Stutthof camp. Until 1944, the prisoners were mostly non-Jewish Poles. Other prisoners included Polish Jews from WARSAW and BIALYSTOK, SOVIET PRISONERS OF WAR, Norwegians, and Danes. In 1944, large number of Jews arrived, mainly from LABOR CAMPS in the Baltic region. They were moved as Soviet troops began to approach. A special camp for German political prisoners was also established in 1944, after the failure of the PLOT TO KILL HITLER in July.

Conditions in the camp were brutal. Starvation was ever present. The poor hygienic conditions in the camp led to epidemics in the winter of 1942 and again in 1944. Periodically, "selections" (see SELEKTIONEN) took place. Those judged by the SS as too weak or sick to work were killed in the camp's small GAS CHAMBER. Gassing with ZYKLON B gas began there in June 1944. Camp doctors also killed sick or in-

Entrance to the Stutthof camp

jured prisoners in the infirmary. More than 60,000 people died in the camp.

The Germans used Stutthof prisoners as FORCED LABORERS. By 1944, the Stutthof camp became the center of a vast network of labor camps. More than 100 sub-camps of Stutthof were established throughout northern and central Poland. Some prisoners worked in SS-owned businesses, such as the German Armament Works (DAW). In 1944, an airplane factory, utilizing forced labor, was built at Stutthof.

In late 1944 and early 1945, as Soviet forces approached, some 50,000 prisoners were forced on DEATH MARCHES. There were evacuations by both land and sea from the camp. Prisoners were transferred to camps in the interior of the German Reich. Marching in dreadful winter conditions, over 25,000 prisoners died. The SS guards shot prisoners who were unable to keep up.

Soviet forces liberated the main camp at Stutthof in early May 1945.

SUGIHARA, CHIUNE (SEMPO)

(1900–1986) Japanese deputy consul general in LITHUANIA from the fall of 1939 to August 1940. He saved many Jews and is one of the "RIGHTEOUS AMONG THE NATIONS." In a rare display of defiance on a diplomatic level, Sugihara acted on his own to issue Japanese transit visas to thousands of JEWS and non-Jews who had fled into Lithuania from German-occupied POLAND. These precious Japanese visas allowed REFUGEES to travel the complicated route from Europe, eastward across Russia to JAPAN. The refugees believed that they would sail on ships from Japan to safe havens in the western hemisphere.

Sugihara was born into a middle class family in a village near Tokyo in 1900. After he entered Japan's Foreign Service, he studied Russian. His interest in Soviet affairs led to assignments in Scandinavia and the Baltic countries. In the fall of 1939, he was appointed deputy consul in KOVNO (Kaunas), Lithuania.

Sempo Sugihara

When Sugihara took up his new post, Germany had just conquered neighboring Poland. The Soviets had seized control of the bordering lands, BYELORUSSIA and the UKRAINE.

Thousands of refugees fleeing both the conquering armies of Adolf HITLER and the terror of Joseph STALIN poured into Lithuania seeking temporary refuge. However, by June 1940, the Soviets moved into Lithuania. Within days, Lithuania's national government was transformed into a communist assembly. All national institutions and private businesses were quickly closed. Organized religions, Jewish and Christian, were banned. All foreign missions were also ordered closed.

As Sugihara began closing the Japanese Consulate, he was approached by a Dutch Jew, Nathan Gutwirth. Gutwirth was one of many Jewish students who had come to Lithuania to study in its many rabbinic academies. Like his fellow students, Gutwirth feared returning to his country—the NETHERLANDS—because it was occupied by German armies. Gutwirth had already convinced Kovno's acting Dutch consul, Jan Zwartendyk, to issue fictitious entrance visas to the Dutch island of Curaçao in the West Indies. All that Gutwirth and others like

him needed was a visa to enter Japan. From Japan, refugees would be able to arrange boat passage across the Pacific, through the Panama Canal to the Dutch West Indies.

At first, Sugihara was cautious about this scheme. He tried to get permission from the Japanese government. He was told not to issue the transit visas. However, Sugihara was moved by the helpless plight of the refugees and he began to issue visas on his own. Sugihara provided at least 2,100 Japanese transit visas between June and August 1940, to Jews and non-Jewish Poles, just as he was being expelled from Lithuania by the Soviets. At first, Sugihara wrote the visas by hand and used traditional Japanese ink and brushes. However, since so many refugees stood outside his door, he eventually used a rubber stamp.

By the end of August 1940, Sugihara was expelled by the Soviets. During the war, he served in diplomatic posts in PRAGUE, Königsberg and BUCHAREST. However, when he returned to Japan in 1947, he was asked to resign from the diplomatic corps because of his refusal to obey orders in 1940. Many years later, YAD VASHEM awarded him the title of "Righteous Among the Nations."

SURVIVORS, FIRST AND SECOND GENERATION OF

People who lived through the HOLOCAUST in hiding or in CAMPS, and their children, born after the war, who are known as the second generation.

The Nazis' brutal system of terror was meant to ensure that no JEWS survived. Few could have hoped to endure the terrible treatment over a long period of time. Those that did survive were deeply affected by their experience. The personal qualities of individual Jews had little to do with their chances of survival.

Even after the war, the survivors' trauma was not over. Most had to face the fact that they had lost their whole family, and often their whole community. They felt insecure and alone. Many survivors did not want to return to their home towns, since they had become graveyards. Thus, they stayed in DISPLACED PERSONS camps until they were allowed to move to countries such as the UNITED STATES, GREAT BRITAIN, and ISRAEL.

In general, their new societies paid little interest to the war-time experiences of the survivors, and rarely provided any psychological support for them. Most survivors tried to put their memories to one side. They concentrated on helping to build a new country (in the case of Israel), learning a new language and culture, finding work, forming new relationships, and starting families. At the time of the liberation from Nazi rule, the Allied soldiers who found the survivors were sure that very few would be able to make a full recovery and live normal lives again. In fact, the majority of survivors did manage to recover, rebuild their lives, and contribute to their new societies. In recent years, they have been encouraged to talk about and document their lives for the historical record (see TESTIMONIES).

Many studies on the psychology of survivors have been made since the war. A number of symptoms—including depression, anxiety, nightmares, and guilt feelings—have been seen as part of the "survivor syndrome." Psychologists warn, however, that it is difficult to generalize about the broad range of experiences of the survivors and their responses to those experiences.

Studies have also been made of the children of survivors and how they were affected by their parents' experience. It has been found that the parent-child relationship was often affected. For example, the parent's fear of separation can lead to over-protectiveness. Children of survivors have explained that they feel pressured to become high achievers in order to repay in some way their parents for all the losses and suffering that they have endured.

In recent years, children of survivors have begun to meet in support groups, where they exchange experiences. Many such groups have taken on the task of encouraging Holocaust education and, in particular, speaking out against HOLOCAUST DENIAL.

S W A S T I K A

The hooked cross symbol of the NAZI PARTY. The swastika is an ancient symbol. It has been found by archeologists in the ruins of Troy, Egypt, China, and India. Its name comes from the Sanskrit language of India, where the symbol was also used as a sign of fertility. In India it was actually used interchangeably with the Star of David. It was Adolf HITLER's idea to adopt the swastika as the Nazi emblem. As a symbol, the swastika had tremendous power. It

The Belgian Fascist leader, Leon Degrelle, speaking at podium decorated with a swastika

inspired the masses of Nazi followers, and struck terror in the hearts of their victims.

> *Maybe the flag with the black spider on it makes people nervous.*
>
> Marta, in the film version of
> "The Sound of Music"

S W E D E N

Scandinavian country that remained neutral throughout WORLD WAR II. The small Jewish community of 7,000 was well integrated. Most of them lived in the capital, Stockholm. After the rise to power of National Socialism in GERMANY, in 1933, German JEWS tried to flee across the Baltic Sea to Sweden. About 3,000 were allowed in by 1939, but there was a public outcry against what was called "the Jewish invasion." Fear of unemployment and of competition was the main reason for this opposition. It was spearheaded by students who demonstrated in the streets. The government modified its liberal immigration laws and by the beginning of 1938, Jews could no longer enter without a visa.

After KRISTALLNACHT, Jewish organizations managed to obtain 500 visas for CHILDREN (without their parents) and another 150 visas for adults. As news about the fate of Jews under the Nazis began to trickle in, public opinion shifted. This shift was also encouraged by a growing shortage of skilled workers in the country. The first serious anti-Jewish measures that were taken in November 1942 in neighboring NORWAY sent shock-waves throughout Sweden and 900 refugees, who had managed to cross the border illegally, were admitted. In October 1943, news of measures threatened against Danish Jews led the Swedish government to make formal protest to the German authorities. When the Germans did not reply, the Swedish government officially offered asylum to the Jews of DENMARK. Along with some 8,000 Jews, a similar number of non-Jewish Danes were allowed in. The Swedish diplomat,

Jews on a boat on their way from Denmark to Sweden, October 1943

Raoul WALLENBERG, and his colleagues saved tens of thousands of Hungarian Jews from DEPORTATION in the last year of the war. Another Swedish initiative, headed by Count Folke BERNADOTTE of the Swedish Red Cross saved thousands of women in the RAVENSBRÜCK camp in the last weeks of the war.

Immediately after the war, survivors from concentration camps were brought to Sweden by the RED CROSS and the UNITED NATIONS RELIEF AND REHABILITATION ADMINISTRATION. Most of the Scandinavian refugees returned to their countries of origin after the war. Many remained in Sweden, while others left to settle in the United States, Canada and Israel.

S W I T Z E R L A N D

Country in central Europe landlocked between FRANCE, GERMANY, AUSTRIA, and ITALY. On the eve of WORLD WAR II, 25,000 JEWS lived in the country. Switzerland, which remained neutral during the war (as it had done during World War I), was not occupied by Germany. There were no antisemitic actions taken against Swiss Jews.

Because of its central position in Europe and its common borders with Germany and Austria, Switzerland could have provided an escape route to Jews fleeing certain death. However, a number of measures were taken by Switzerland even before the beginning of the war to keep this from happening. German and Austrian tourists did not need a visa to enter Switzerland. However, in 1938, Swiss authorities asked Germany and Austria to put a special mark in the passports of Jews so that the Swiss could deny them entry. Germany and Austria readily

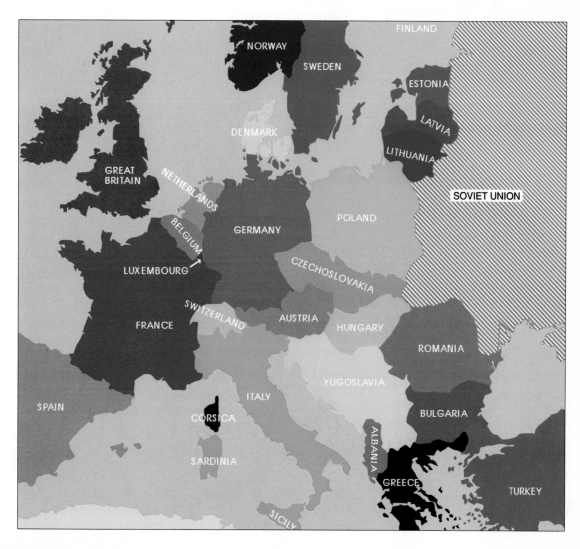

Refugee camp for German Jews in Switzerland, 1940

agreed, and stamped a red "J" on passports of Jews.

Switzerland had traditionally been a land of refuge, but now it was concerned not to give Germany an excuse to invade it. Shortly after the war broke out, restrictions were imposed on the entry of refugees, especially Jews. Those who were allowed in were put in camps. Although the restrictions were relaxed under certain circumstances (for example many refugees from Belgium and the Netherlands were admitted in 1941), they were made more severe at other times. This was especially the case after the Germans took over southern France in November 1942. Then, the Swiss blocked the escape route of thousands of Jews trying to flee from the Germans. In the fall of 1943—with the Germans in effect occupying Italy—Switzerland did allow in 74,000 foreigners, most of them Italians and including a few thousand Jews. Over 1,000 Jewish orphans from France were allowed in at the end of 1943. In 1944, there was a further relaxation and by the end of the year, the total number of refugees living in Switzerland exceeded 100,000. However, it is estimated that some 10,000 refugees were turned back at the border

into the hands of the Germans during the war. The officials at the borders used the code phrase "The Boat is Full" to indicate that they had no room for more refugees. On some occasions, those turned away committed suicide on the spot—rather than go back to the Germans.

During the war, some 300,000 foreigners were allowed into Switzerland, although the country tried to ensure that as many as possible moved on to other destinations. This total included some 30,000 Jews. Support for the Jewish refugees was provided by the AMERICAN JEWISH JOINT DISTRIBUTION COMMITTEE (Joint), HICEM, and by the Swiss Jewish community.

A number of world Jewish organizations, such as the Joint and the WORLD JEWISH CONGRESS, had offices in Geneva during the war.

SZÁLASI, FERENC

(1897–1946) Leader of the Hungarian fascist ARROW CROSS Party. A retired major in the Hungarian Army, he formed the Nazi-type Hungarian Party of Resolve and later the Hungarist Movement. Convicted of subversion, he was sentenced to three years in prison but was released in 1940. Ferenc Szálasi promptly organized the Arrow Cross Party, which used the arrow cross as its symbol. His following came chiefly from the unemployed, the impoverished gentry, and a few intellectuals and aristocrats. His program was rabidly antisemitic, demanding severe restrictive measures against the JEWS. When the Hungarian regent, Admiral Miklós HORTHY, was removed by the Germans, Adolf HITLER appointed Szálasi head of state on 15 October 1944.

On 20 October, a reign of terror began in BUDAPEST against the Jews. 76,000 men, women and CHILDREN were rounded up and marched on foot toward the German frontier. Those unable to keep up were shot or died of exhaustion and starvation (see DEATH MARCH). Most of the remaining Jews were shut into the ghetto, where many were robbed, killed on the spot, and 10,000–20,000 were marched to the banks of the Danube river and shot there. When the German-Hungarian garrison surrendered to the Russians on 13 February 1945, Szálasi fled. He was captured by the Americans in GERMANY and was returned to Budapest to be tried for war crimes and CRIMES AGAINST HUMANITY. He was sentenced to death and publicly hanged in 1946.

SZENES, HANNA

(1921–1944) Jewish Zionist activist, poet and PALESTINE-based paratrooper during WORLD WAR II. She was born into an assimilated Hungarian Jewish family.

Hungarian JEWS experienced intense antisemitism during Szenes's teens (see HUNGARY). She became a devoted Zionist, and moved to Palestine in 1939. In 1943, Szenes volunteered to be part of a special military unit organized by the Haganah (Jewish defense force in Palestine) and British intelligence. It was composed of 32 Palestinian Jews. The parachutists' mission was to enter Nazi-occupied Europe to organize .movements, aid escaped Allied prisoners of war, collect and send intelligence reports and help to rescue Jewish survivors. Szenes's group parachuted into YUGOSLAVIA in the late spring of 1944. She entered Hungary that June and was captured almost immediately. She was imprisoned in Budapest and tortured, but she did not give away any information.

In November 1944, the Hungarian FASCISTS held a

Hannah Szenes's last poem, written in prison in Budapest

One — two — three...
eight feet long,
Two strides across, the rest is dark...
Life hangs over me like a question mark.

One — two — three...
maybe another week,
Or next month may still find me here,
But death, I feel, is very near.
I could have been
twenty-three next July;
I gambled on what mattered most,
The dice were cast. I lost.

Budapest, 1944

---

court martial to try Szenes for treason. She was convicted of espionage and executed late in November 1944. Her remains were moved to Israel in 1950 and she was buried on Mount Herzl, Jerusalem, Israel's national military cemetery.

Hannah Szenes and her brother Giora in Palestine

index

Darkened numbers indicate an entry on the subject in this volume